Focus in Prekindergarten

Teaching with Curriculum Focal Points

Additional titles in the
Teaching with Curriculum Focal Points series:

The Teaching with Curriculum Focal Points series consists of grade-level publications designed to support teachers, supervisors, and coordinators as they begin the discussion of a more focused curriculum across and within prekindergarten through grade 8, as presented in *Curriculum Focal Points for Prekindergarten through Grade 8 Mathematics*.

	ISBN #	NCTM stock #
Focus in Kindergarten	978-0-87353-645-5	13627
Focus in Grade 1	978-0-87353-646-2	13628
Focus in Grade 2	Coming Fall 2010	
Focus in Pre-K–2	978-0-87353-624-0	13486
Focus in Grade 3	978-0-87353-625-7	13487
Focus in Grade 4	978-0-87353-627-1	13490
Focus in Grade 5	978-0-87353-614-1	13437
Focus in Grades 3–5	978-0-87353-609-7	13395
Focus in Grade 6	978-0-87353-648-6	13630
Focus in Grade 7	978-0-87353-649-3	13631
Focus in Grade 8	978-0-87353-650-9	13632
Focus in Grades 6–8	978-0-87353-618-9	13465

Please visit www.nctm.org/catalog for details and ordering information.

Focus in Prekindergarten

Teaching with Curriculum Focal Points

Planning and Writing Team

Karen C. Fuson, *Chair, Northwestern University (Professor Emerita)*

Douglas H. Clements, *University at Buffalo, State University of New York*

Sybilla Beckmann, *University of Georgia*

NATIONAL COUNCIL OF
TEACHERS OF MATHEMATICS

National Association for the
Education of Young Children

Copyright © 2010 by
THE NATIONAL COUNCIL OF TEACHERS OF MATHEMATICS, INC.
1906 Association Drive, Reston, VA 20191-1502
(703) 620-9840; (800) 235-7566; www.nctm.org
All rights reserved

Published simultaneously by the National Council of Teachers of Mathematics and by
the National Association for the Education of Young Children, 1313 L Street, NW,
Suite 500, Washington DC 20005-4101, www.naeyc.org.

Library of Congress Cataloging-in-Publication Data

Fuson, Karen C.
    Focus in prekindergarten : teaching with curriculum focal points / Planning and Writing Team,
Karen C. Fuson, Douglas H. Clements, Sybilla Beckmann.
        p. cm.
    Includes bibliographical references.
    ISBN 978-0-87353-644-8 (alk. paper)
    1. Mathematics—Study and teaching (Preschool)—United States—Standards. 2. Education,
Preschool—Curricula—United States—Standards. 3. Curriculum planning—United States—
Standards. I. Fuson, Karen C. II. Clements, Douglas H. III. Beckmann, Sybilla. IV. Title: Focus
in prekindergarten
    QA135.6.F874 2009
    372.7—dc22
                                                                        2009044378

The National Council of Teachers of Mathematics is a public voice of mathematics education,
supporting teachers to ensure equitable mathematics learning of the highest quality for all students
through vision, leadership, professional development, and research.

Printed in the United States of America

Contents

Contents — Continued

PREFACE

On September 12, 2006, the National Council of Teachers of Mathematics released *Curriculum Focal Points for Prekindergarten through Grade 8 Mathematics: A Quest for Coherence* to encourage discussions at the national, state, and district levels on the importance of designing a coherent elementary mathematics curriculum focusing on the important mathematical ideas at each grade level. The natural question that followed the release of *Curriculum Focal Points* was "How do we translate this view of a focused curriculum into the classroom?"

Focus in Prekindergarten, one in a series of grade-level publications, is designed to support teachers, supervisors, and coordinators as they begin the discussion of a more focused curriculum across and within prekindergarten through eighth grade, as presented in *Curriculum Focal Points.* Additionally, teacher educators should find it useful as a vehicle for exploring mathematical ideas and curriculum issues involving the prekindergarten mathematics curriculum with their preservice teachers.

The members of the planning and writing team, all active leaders in mathematics education and professional development, created this grade-level book as a framework for individual or group experiences in which teachers deepen their understanding of the mathematical ideas they will be teaching. This book describes and illustrates learning paths for the mathematical concepts and skills of each prekindergarten Focal Point, including powerful representational supports for teaching and learning that can facilitate understanding, stimulate productive discussions about mathematical thinking, and provide a foundation for fluency with the core ideas. We also discuss common student errors and misconceptions, reasons the errors may arise, and teaching methods or visual representations to address the errors. Because learning paths cut across grades, we have included some discussion of related Focal Points at kindergarten and grade 1 so that we can describe and clarify prerequisite knowledge in prekindergarten that contributes to later understandings.

Whether you are working with your colleagues or individually, we hope you will find the discussions of the learning paths, representations, and lines of reasoning valuable as you plan activities and discussions for your students and as you strive to help your students achieve the depth of understanding of important mathematical concepts necessary for their future success.

—Karen C. Fuson, *Chair*
Douglas H. Clements
Sybilla Beckmann
Prekindergarten Planning and Writing Team

As states and local school districts implement more rigorous assessment and accountability systems, teachers often face long lists of mathematics topics or learning expectations to address at each grade level, with many topics repeating from year to year. Lacking clear, consistent priorities and focus, teachers stretch to find the time to present important mathematical topics effectively and in depth.

The National Council of Teachers of Mathematics (NCTM) is responding to this challenge by presenting *Curriculum Focal Points for Prekindergarten through Grade 8 Mathematics: A Quest for Coherence*. Building on *Principles and Standards for School Mathematics* (NCTM 2000), this new publication is offered as a starting point in a dialogue on what is important at particular levels of instruction and as an initial step toward a more coherent, focused curriculum in this country.

The writing team for *Curriculum Focal Points for Prekindergarten through Grade 8 Mathematics* consisted of nine members, with at least one university-level mathematics educator or mathematician and one pre-K–8 classroom practitioner from each of the three grade bands (pre-K–grade 2, grades 3–5, and grades 6–8). The writing team examined curricula from multiple states and countries as well as a wide array of researchers' and experts' writings in creating a set of focal points for pre-K–grade 8 mathematics.

On behalf of the Board of Directors, we thank everyone who helped make this publication possible.

Cathy Seeley
President, 2004–2006
National Council of Teachers of Mathematics

Francis (Skip) Fennell
President, 2006–2008
National Council of Teachers of Mathematics

Members of the Curriculum Focal Points for Grades PK–8 Writing Team

Jane F. Schielack, *Chair*, Texas A&M University, College Station, Texas
Sybilla Beckmann, University of Georgia, Athens, Georgia
Randall I. Charles, San José State University (emeritus), San José, California
Douglas H. Clements, University at Buffalo, State University of New York, Buffalo, New York
Paula B. Duckett, District of Columbia Public Schools (retired), Washington, D.C.
Francis (Skip) Fennell, McDaniel College, Westminster, Maryland
Sharon L. Lewandowski, Bryant Woods Elementary School, Columbia, Maryland
Emma Treviño, Charles A. Dana Center, University of Texas at Austin, Austin, Texas
Rose Mary Zbiek, The Pennsylvania State University, University Park, Pennsylvania

Staff Liaison
Melanie S. Ott, National Council of Teachers of Mathematics, Reston, Virginia

ACKNOWLEDGMENTS

The National Council of Teachers of Mathematics would like to thank Sue Bredekamp, DeAnn Huinker, and Henry S. Kepner Jr. for thoughtful and helpful comments on drafts of the manuscript. Special thanks are due to Francis (Skip) Fennell for initiating the project and for his enthusiastic support and encouragement, and to Henry S. Kepner Jr. for continuing to carry the Focal Points torch with equal dedication and support.

The final product reflects the editorial expertise of Ann M. Butterfield, NCTM senior editor, and the design expertise of Randy White, NCTM production manager.

1 Introduction

Purpose of This Guide

Special aspects of prekindergarten mathematics for all students

In prekindergarten and even in kindergarten, goals for children in mathematics are too limited and do not include goals that children can and should learn. On the basis of prior experiences, many children come to prekindergarten (pre-K) and kindergarten (K) with a wide range of mathematical knowledge. Other children—often, but not exclusively, associated with experiences living in poverty and other equity conditions—come with much less mathematical knowledge. This mathematics gap can be closed with effective targeted learning experiences in mathematics before school. A major report by the National Research Council (NRC) Committee on Early Childhood Math (Cross, Woods, and Schweingruber 2009) summarizes the research concerning these issues. The title of the report is *Mathematics Learning in Early Childhood: Paths toward Excellence and Equity*. This title emphasizes that the report identifies foundational and achievable learning goals for pre-K, K, and grade 1. The report also discusses effective approaches for teaching that can lead to equity.

Curriculum Focal Points for Prekindergarten through Grade 8 Mathematics: A Quest for Coherence (NCTM 2006) was developed to address a major national issue: a lack of clear, consistent priorities and focus of mathematics standards by grade level in the United States. Each state, and often each district within a state, has its own set of mathematics goals. Across states, a particular goal can vary as much as three years (e.g., from grade 3 to grade 5). Also, most states have too many goals. The *Focal Points* are a major step toward establishing coherence and a consistent set of expectations for children in the United States.

The NRC committee used the NCTM *Curriculum Focal Points* as one of the bases of its work on the goals. It recommends that all Pre-K and K work concentrate on the three topics reflected in *Curriculum Focal Points:* number and operations, geometry, and measurement. The NRC committee recommended that number and operations be the primary goal. Focused time is needed on geometry as a primary goal, but for less class time. Although measurement ideas at these grades are important, the NRC recommended that only a small amount of time is needed for them. Work on patterns and data can be woven into work on these topics, but not with the same time investment. It is important to note that experiences that address more than one of these topic areas can facilitate learning and deepen understanding. For example, a geometry-focused activity can involve number, and vice versa.

Curriculum Focal Points and the NRC report are major efforts that deserve to be coordinated. The writing team for this book served on the NRC Early Childhood Math Committee, and two of the writers also served on the committee that developed the Focal Points. The Focal Points are too brief to provide effective guidance for multiage or whole grade levels. The writing team examined the goals from the NRC Early Childhood Math Report and integrated them into the expanded Focal Points tables used in this book.

Both *Curriculum Focal Points* and the NRC report emphasize coordinated learning paths through which children move within and across grades. The tables in this book show goals for successive grades that build on the pre-K teaching and learning. This clarifies for pre-K teachers and other educators how foundational and necessary it is for them to work deeply on the pre-K mathematics goals outlined here. Only when all children have opportunities to learn these goals can they enter kindergarten ready for the goals at that level. As the NRC report concluded, it is vital to close the gap between those children with such opportunities and those without by providing effective teaching and learning experiences before kindergarten.

The core mathematical ideas discussed in this book are mathematically central and coherent. They are a necessary foundation for important mathematical ideas that come later. They are consistent with children's ways of thinking, developing, and learning. They are generative of future learning and are engaging and interesting to children.

We address the prekindergarten period in two parts:

- two- and three-year-olds (called 2s/3s for brevity), and

- four-year-olds or those children who will enter kindergarten in the following year (called 4s/pre-Ks for brevity).

The goals and learning experiences described in this book are appropriate for parents to do in the home, for caregivers in child care settings, or for teachers in schools.

Learning Similarities across Number and Operations, Geometry, and Measurement

Mathematics is powerful because it unifies a wide variety of situations and applies to many different examples. To tap into the power of mathematics, children must *mathematize* the situations they encounter. For example, children mathematize when they notice that there are three squirrels rather than just "some squirrels," when they see that they need to get exactly two more spoons so that everyone will have one, or when they observe that a paper napkin is in the shape of a square but a tissue is not. To mathematize is to focus on the mathematical aspects of a situation and then to formulate that situation in mathematical terms; it is a means for children to deepen, extend, elaborate, and refine their thinking as they explore ideas and lines of reasoning. When children mathematize their experiences, they solve problems; they reason and communicate their reasoning; they represent ideas using objects, drawings, written symbols, or internal visualization; and they connect ideas. When children mathematize, they use mathematics to help make sense of the world and they also build their knowledge of mathematics itself. They develop and use special "math eyes" that see the mathematics in the world, and they learn the mathematics language that describes those mathematical aspects.

In addition to the general processes of representing, reasoning, communicating, connecting, and problem solving, specific mathematical reasoning processes also exist that are important across all topics in mathematics, and that mathematics instruction should help children develop. These processes are—

- *unitizing*—finding or creating a unit, such as joining 10 ones to create a unit of ten, or recognizing that a repeating pattern *ababab...* is created by repeating the unit *ab;*

- *decomposing and composing,* such as putting six triangles together in a special way to make a hexagon, decomposing a square into two triangles, or decomposing seven toy dinosaurs into a group of five and a group of two;

- *relating and ordering,* such as putting a collection of sticks in order by length or determining which collection of bears has more by matching; and

- *looking for patterns and structures and organizing information,* such as noticing that two and three more must be the same amount as three and two more or sorting a collection of shapes according to how many sides the shapes have.

The Need for Focused Mathematics Teaching Time in Pre-K

Understanding the mathematics content and becoming fluent in using the mathematics process goals require many repeated experiences with the same numbers or same shapes and related similar tasks. Mathematics is a participant sport. Young children must play it frequently to become good at it. They also need modeling of correct performance, discussion about the concepts involved, and feedback about their performance. Both modeling and feedback can come from their peers as well as from adults, and feedback also sometimes comes from the situation. For example, children are often better at seeing counting errors when other children make them than when they make them, and they can respond to an adult's request to "show three fingers" by looking at peers if they do not know. If they are counting out spoons to take to the table, they will find out they have too many or too few when they lay the spoons at the places where people sit.

All children must have sustained and frequent times in which they themselves engage in important mathematical ideas and talk about what they are doing and why they are doing it. In mathematics learning, effort creates ability.

The NRC report recommends that home, child care, preschool, and school environments need to support children in the process of becoming self-initiating and self-guiding learners. When children have opportunities to move along the learning paths described for each Focal Point, they become interested in consolidating and extending their knowledge. They begin to practice by themselves. They seek out additional information by asking questions and giving themselves new tasks, if given the opportunity in their environment.

Targeted learning-path time for specific mathematics goals is crucial. Children need time and support to consolidate thinking at one step and to move along the learning path to the next step. It is not enough to weave mathematics into other activities, although integrating mathematics can be a part of many learning opportunities. Children need enough time to focus on the goals discussed in this book if they are to gain understanding and fluency in them. Even children who learn mathematical ideas at home will benefit from a consistent high-quality program experience in the preschool and kindergarten years. Time must be allocated for more formal parts of mathematics instruction and discussions that occur in whole groups or in small groups and for plenty of follow-up practice. Practice does not mean rote experiences. Practice involves repeated experiences that give children time and opportunity to build their ideas, develop understanding, and increase fluency. Children also need time to elaborate and extend their mathematical thinking by exploring and sharing their own methods.

Research reviewed in the NRC report indicates that at least twenty to thirty minutes a day are needed for children to learn the goals in this book. More time is helpful, especially for children who enter school with relatively little mathematical knowledge. As will become clear in the next section, appropriate learning experiences in mathematics also support language development and real-life knowledge, so some of this mathematics time is accomplishing language goals.

Effective Teaching-Learning Practices

Children can be powerful and intrinsically motivated mathematics learners if they experience a supportive physical and social environment. Children need adult guidance to help them learn the many culturally important aspects of mathematics, such as language and counting. In preschools and care centers, all children bring to each mathematical topic some initial competencies and knowledge on which to build. The major teaching challenge is to build a physical and social mathematical learning and teaching environment in which all children have explicit experiences and support to learn the goals for each topic area and continue to practice and build on their own knowledge, with guidance from adults, peers, and family members.

Aspects of effective teaching-learning practices are outlined in table 1.1. Most of them have been mentioned in the foregoing. They are summarized to emphasize that the need for focused mathematics teaching time goes well beyond a single approach. It does not mean all teacher showing and telling or an emphasis on worksheets. Parts A and B of table 1.1 emphasize the two ongoing vital roles of teachers:

A. expect and support children's ability to make meaning and mathematize the real world, and

B. create a nurturing and helping math-talk community.

Part C reiterates the need for a teacher to lead the class through a research-based learning path based on children's thinking, as outlined in tables 2.1 and 3.1 and discussed in this book. An important part of such learning paths is that they provide repeated meaningful experience with core concepts so that young children can truly learn in depth. Such learning requires focusing more deeply on fewer topics, a crucial aspect of the Focal Point goals presented and discussed here. Just as hearing a story repeatedly is interesting to young children, so too young children are interested in repeatedly reciting the list of number words, repeatedly counting collections of objects, and repeatedly putting shapes together to make new shapes. And just as hearing a story anew gives children new insights and a deeper understanding of the story, so too repeated counting and repeated examination of shapes help children develop new insights and a deeper understanding of mathematical ideas.

Table 1.1
Effective Teaching-Learning Practices

A. The teacher expects and supports *children's ability to make meaning and mathematize* the real world by—
   - providing *settings that connect* mathematical language and symbols to quantities and to actions in the world,
   - *leading children's attention* across these crucial aspects to help them see patterns and make connections, and
   - *supporting repeated experiences* that give children time and opportunity to build their ideas, develop understanding, and increase fluency.

B. The teacher creates a nurturing and helping *math-talk community*—
   - within which to *elicit thinking* from students, and
   - to help students *explain and help* each other explain and solve problems.

C. For each big mathematics topic, the teacher leads the class through a research-*based learning path* based on children's thinking. Doing so allows the teacher to differentiate instruction within whole-class, small-group, and center-based activities. This path provides the repeated experiences that young children need.

D. For later pre-K and K, children need to follow up activities with real three-dimensional objects by working with mathematics drawings and other written two-dimensional representations that *support practice and meaning-making with written mathematical symbols.* Children of all ages also need to see and count groups of things in books, that is, they need to experience and understand three-dimensional things as pictures on a two-dimensional surface. Working with and on two-dimensional surfaces, as well as with three-dimensional objects, supports equity in mathematics literacy because some children have not had experiences with two-dimensional representations in their out-of-school environment.

Part D emphasizes the importance of relating children's work with quantities and objects in the real world to pictures of these in books and on other two-dimensional surfaces or pieces of paper. Doing so is especially important for children coming from homes where such experiences are infrequent or nonexistent. In later prekindergarten and in kindergarten, it is also important to help children relate real three-dimensional objects to mathematics drawings of those objects and to written mathematics symbols. At these ages, all children need to have both kinds of experiences: with actual objects and things and with mathematics drawings and symbols of the things. And both of these kinds of experiences need to reflect the teaching-learning practices A, B, and C. At present, too many children have only one kind of experience, which often is linked to children's background. Too many children in pre-K settings, many from backgrounds of poverty, experience only or primarily worksheets that support rote learning, and too many children from backgrounds of affluence experience only or primarily work with objects not related to mathematics drawings or symbols, reducing the meanings they can make. Early childhood educators rightfully object to the use of worksheets only to assess what children already know. However, worksheets (activities on paper) can support understanding and increase fluency if they are used after the experiences with objects, relate to those experiences, and are used by adults focusing on teaching-learning practices A and B: meaning making and mathematizing and creating a math-talk community. Worksheets can stimulate discussions of mathematizing in the real world and of visual patterns that are important mathematically. They can also provide practice, reflection, and experience with seeing things and drawing on paper. The real issue is not worksheets versus objects. It is supporting meaning-making, mathematizing, and making connections among mathematical language, symbols, and quantities and shapes.

Table 1.1 outlines effective teaching-learning practices by teachers in centers of various kinds. The same practices are important for parents when they help their child learn mathematical ideas at home or out in the world. Parents can do all aspects of part A and do supportive math talk as outlined in part B. They can expect and support their child's ability to make meaning and mathematize the real world by talking about mathematical ideas they see in the world and helping their child talk about those ideas by extending their child's language and practicing seeing and counting small numbers of things. Parents can do part D by discussing mathematical ideas in books with their child (e.g., "How many foxes are on this page?" or "What shapes make this house?"). More examples are given throughout the book.

Organization of This Book

The rest of this book is in three sections. The original brief Focal Points for pre-K appear first, and then the detailed goals table begins each of the two Focal Point sections. The language in the detailed tables sometimes has been modified from the original Focal Point language to be clearer and to reflect the goals and language in the NRC report. The final section overviews mathematizing.

Curriculum Focal Points and Connections for Prekindergarten

The set of three curriculum focal points and related connections for mathematics in prekindergarten follow. These topics are the recommended content emphases for this grade level. It is essential that these focal points be addressed in contexts that promote problem solving, reasoning, communication, making connections, and designing and analyzing representations.

Prekindergarten Curriculum Focal Points	Connections to the Focal Points
Number and Operations: Developing an understanding of whole numbers, including concepts of correspondence, counting, cardinality, and comparison Children develop an understanding of the meanings of whole numbers and recognize the number of objects in small groups without counting and by counting—the first and most basic mathematical algorithm. They understand that number words refer to quantity. They use one-to-one correspondence to solve problems by matching sets and comparing number amounts and in counting objects to 10 and beyond. They understand that the last word that they state in counting tells "how many," they count to determine number amounts and compare quantities (using language such as "more than" and "less than"), and they order sets by the number of objects in them.	*Data Analysis:* Children learn the foundations of data analysis by using objects' attributes that they have identified in relation to geometry and measurement (e.g., size, quantity, orientation, number of sides or vertices, color) for various purposes, such as describing, sorting, or comparing. For example, children sort geometric figures by shape, compare objects by weight ("heavier," "lighter"), or describe sets of objects by the number of objects in each set. *Number and Operations:* Children use meanings of numbers to create strategies for solving problems and responding to practical situations, such as getting just enough napkins for a group, or mathematical situations, such as determining that any shape is a triangle if it has exactly three straight sides and is closed. *Algebra:* Children recognize and duplicate simple sequential patterns (e.g., square, circle, square, circle, square, circle, …).
Geometry: Identifying shapes and describing spatial relationships Children develop spatial reasoning by working from two perspectives on space as they examine the shapes of objects and inspect their relative positions. They find shapes in their environments and describe them in their own words. They build pictures and designs by combining two- and three-dimensional shapes, and they solve such problems as deciding which piece will fit into a space in a puzzle. They discuss the relative positions of objects with vocabulary such as "above," "below," and "next to."	
Measurement: Identifying measurable attributes and comparing objects by using these attributes Children identify objects as "the same" or "different," and then "more" or "less," on the basis of attributes that they can measure. They identify measurable attributes such as length and weight and solve problems by making direct comparisons of objects on the basis of those attributes.	

Reprinted from *Curriculum Focal Points for Prekindergarten through Grade 8 Mathematics: A Quest for Coherence* (Reston, Va.: NCTM, 2006, p. 11).

Overview of Number and Operations

The topic of number and operations has three major components: the number core, the relations core, and the operations core.

◆ The *number core* focuses on four components:

- seeing cardinality (seeing how many there are),
- knowing the number word list (one, two, three, four, etc.),
- one-to-one counting correspondences when counting, and
- written number symbols (1, 2, 3, etc.).

◆ The *relations core* concerns finding the relationship between two groups of objects or two numbers: Is one of these more than, or less than, or equal to the other?

◆ The *operations core* involves adding or subtracting two groups of objects or numbers to make a third.

The numbers in the number-word list are always larger than the numbers children can work with in the other three aspects of the number core. Children need to have said an accurate number-word list many times. They need to be able to say it very easily because they need mental capacity to do other things while they say it, for example, point at objects with one-to-one correspondence or remember a number to which they are counting.

The Number Core: Early 2s/3s

Overview

The number core for children just beginning to learn about numbers focuses on four components of very small numbers (1, 2, 3):

- seeing cardinality (seeing how many there are),
- knowing the number word list (one, two, three, four, etc.),
- one-to-one counting correspondences when counting, and
- written number symbols (1, 2, 3).

Initially these four aspects are separate, and then children make vital connections. To count objects, they connect saying the number word list with one-to-one correspondences. At first, this counting is just an activity; children do not understand that the last word is special, that it tells them the total amount (its cardinality). If asked the question "How many are there?" after a child has counted, she or he may count again (repeatedly) or give a number word different from the last counted word. Connecting counting and cardinality is a crucial step in the learning path that coordinates the first three aspects of the number core. This step occurs at the next level, later 2s/3s.

Table 2.1

Progression of Ideas about Number and Operations (and Algebra from Kindergarten On)

Prekindergarten	Kindergarten	Grade 1
The Number Core	**The Number Core**	**The Number Core**
2s/3s: Learn these four number-core components for very small numbers (1, 2, 3): seeing cardinality (seeing how many there are), knowing the number-word list, one-to-one counting correspondences when counting, and written number symbols. Later, coordinate these components to count up to six things and say the number counted as the cardinality. Also extend the core components to larger numbers: sometimes seeing four or five, saying the number-word list to ten, reading numerals 1 through 5. 4s/pre-Ks: Count out *n* things (up to 10), see numbers 6 to 10 with a 5-group (dot arrays, fingers) and extend the core components to larger numbers: say the number-word list to thirty-nine, count seven to fifteen things in a row, and read numerals 1 to 10 and work on writing some numerals.	Integrate all core components for teen numbers (10 to 19) to see a ten and some ones in teen numbers (e.g., 18 = 10 + 8) and relate 10 ones to 1 ten. Extend the core components: say the tens list 10, 20, …, 100 and count to 100 by ones, count up to twenty-five things in a row with effort, read and write 1 to 19.	See, say, count, draw, and write tens-units and ones-units from 1 to 100, seeing and counting the groups of ten both as decades (ten, twenty, thirty, …) and as tens (1 ten, 2 tens, 3 tens, …).
The Relations (More Than/Less Than) Core	**The Relations (More Than/Less Than) Core**	**The Relations (More Than/Less Than) Core**
2s/3s: Use perceptual, length, and density strategies to find *which is more* for two numbers ≤ 5. 4s/pre-Ks: Use counting and matching strategies to find *which is more* for two numbers ≤ 5 and begin also to use *less/fewer*.	Show comparing situations with objects or in a drawing, and match or count to find out *which is more* and *which is less* for two numbers ≤ 10. Use = and ≠ symbols for groups of things, numerals, and pictures of fingers.	Solve additive comparison word problems that ask "How many more (less) is one group than another?" for two numbers ≤ 18 by counting or matching with objects or drawings or by knowing numerical relationships (such word problems describe relations between two numbers more precisely: the difference is now involved). Use the words *more/fewer-less* and > and < to compare numbers to 10 and use the concepts of tens and ones developed in the number core and multiunit objects or math drawings to compare numbers to 100.

The Operations (Addition/Subtraction) Core	The Operations (Addition/Subtraction) Core	The Operations (Addition/Subtraction) Core
2s/3s: Solve situation problems and oral number problems with totals ≤ 5: act out with objects change-plus, change-minus, and put-together/take-apart situations. 4s/pre-Ks: Use objects or fingers or pictures to solve the foregoing situation problems, word problems, and oral number problems with totals ≤ 8. Work on decomposing 3, 4, 5 in partners (5 has 4 and 1 and also 3 and 2 hiding inside it).	Use objects or fingers or pictures or mathematics drawings to solve change-plus, change-minus, and put-together/take-apart situation problems and also such word, oral number, and written symbolic problems with totals ≤ 10. Pose as well as solve such problems. Learn to decompose 3, 4, 5, into partners; work on decomposing 6 and 7 (e.g., $6 = 5 + 1$, $6 = 4 + 2$, $6 = 3 + 3$, $6 = 2 + 4$, $6 = 1 + 5$); see equations with one number on the left and the partners (addends) on the right.	Use objects or fingers or mathematics drawings and equations to solve change-plus, change-minus, and put-together/take-apart situation problems with all unknowns and also such word, oral number, and written symbolic problems with addends from 1 to 9. Pose as well as solve such problems. After working with additive comparison situations and word problems (see the relations core above), mix all types of word problems. Learn to decompose numbers from 3 to 10 into partners (e.g., $10 = 9 + 1$, $10 = 8 + 2$, $10 = 7 + 3$, $10 = 6 + 4$, $10 = 5 + 5$) and use these relationships to relate addition and subtraction in problem situations, to add and subtract quickly for totals ≤ 6, and to build the prerequisite knowledge for addition and subtraction strategies. Count on for addition problems with totals ≤ 18 and find subtraction as an unknown addend by counting on fluently and accurately (think of and rewrite $14 − 8 = ?$ as $8 + ? = 14$). Work with derived fact strategies such as make-a-ten and doubles +1 or −1. Give unknown totals or unknown addends (subtraction) quickly for totals ≤ 6 and for +1 and −1 for totals ≤10. Use the concepts of tens and ones developed in the number core and use multiunit objects or mathematics drawings to add and subtract tens and ones (e.g., $60 + 3$) and tens and tens (e.g., $40 + 20$) and to add two-digit numbers and ones (e.g., $58 + 6$) and 2 two-digit numbers starting with problems requiring regrouping (e.g., $38 + 26$) (do not do such subtraction problems with or without regrouping). Relate math drawings to written number (symbolic) work.

Sees cardinality (seeing how many there are) for 1, 2, 3

Children's knowledge of cardinality (how many are in a set) increases as they learn specific number words for sets of objects they see (e.g., I want two crackers.). Children may at first have several different contexts in which they use the word *one* or *two*. *Two* might mean *one* (e.g., cracker, cookie) in each hand or two identical things right beside each other (e.g., two cups). Only later do these special meanings of *two* collapse into the same meaning. Parents and caregivers need to say a number word for many different examples of things so that young children learn to mathematize their environment: look for and see numerical aspects and say a number word for what they see.

We do not really know the process by which children (and adults) see cardinalities for very small numbers. Birds and primates also can see cardinalities and can say or choose a sign or symbol for them. For humans, the process of such verbal labeling can begin even before age two. This process does have a name, *subitizing* or *perceptual subitizing,* that the reader may see in articles about early number learning.

Children first label objects that they can see, and later they label non-present objects visualized mentally (see sidebar "Early Uses of the Word *Two*"). This step of naming a cardinality (how many there are) is the crucial first step in understanding cardinality. It needs to be supported frequently in the home and in care and educational centers.

Children also learn to assign a number to sets of entities they hear but do not see, such as drum beats or ringing bells. For example, on the fourth of July, a child might say, "Daddy, I hear three cracker-fires!" Such auditory quantities relate to music and rhythm and to body movements. Children can repeat simple sets they hear (clap-clap or clap-clap-clap), tell the number they hear (e.g., of bells, drumbeats, feet stamping, etc.), and produce sounds with body movements for particular quantities (e.g., "Let me hear three claps").

In home and care or educational settings, it is important that early experiences seeing and saying cardinalities use simple objects or pictures and later extend to more complex objects or pictures. Children who spontaneously focus on seeing cardinality are more skilled at later counting and arithmetic skills. Asking children to tell how many ___ they see often throughout the day is crucially important. This can be done, for example, in small-group situations where children each have a card with one, two, or three pictures on it. Each child says how many he or she sees on a card, and then the cards are rotated and each child replies again until everyone has done each card. The adult models and helps as needed. Children move from just saying the number to saying a whole sentence, for example, "I see three dogs." Saying the full sentence should be modeled and encouraged. Asking "How many?" also can happen informally throughout the day, for example, when reading a book (e.g., "How many ducks are in the pond?") or giving snacks ("Here are two pieces of apple. How many pieces of apple?" ["Two"]).

Research has also found that adults can increase children's spontaneous focusing, and doing so leads to better competence in cardinality tasks. Increasing children's spontaneous focusing on seeing cardinalities is an example of helping children mathematize their environment, that is, see (develop "math eyes"), seek out, and use the mathematical information in it. Such tendencies can stimulate children's self-initiated practice in numerical skills because they notice those features and are interested in them. Therefore children will need specific learning opportunities to see cardinalities and label them with a number word, but they also need to learn to do so spontaneously in their home and care or educational setting. It is important for families to support such seeing of "How many?" at home.

Says number-word list accurately to six

Children begin to learn the ordered list of number words as a sort of chant separate from any use of that list in counting objects or in labeling cardinalities (how many there are). Some children even confuse numbers and letters initially because these are just two different meaningless lists for them. For example, a child might say walking up the stairs: "A, B, C, four, five, six."

Families and teachers say the number-word list, and children repeat as much of it as they can remember. Very early lists may be out of order, but very soon the errors take on a typical form. Children typically say the first part of the list correctly and then may omit some numbers within the next portion of the list, or say a lot of numbers out of order, often repeating them (e.g., "one, two, three, eight, nine, four, five, two, six"). Children need many opportunities to hear a correct number list to include the missing numbers and to extend the list (see sidebar "Helping Children Learn the Number-Word List" for examples).

Children can learn and practice the number-word list by hearing and by saying it without doing anything else, or it can be heard or said in coordination with an action like jumping or climbing stairs. Saying it alone allows the child to concentrate on the words, and later on the patterns in the words. Saying the words with actions (for example, tapping the head or pointing out or shaking a finger) can add interest and facilitate the one-to-one correspondences in counting objects. Accuracy in saying the number word list is not enough. The child has to be able to say the list easily to be able to say it while counting objects.

Counting: one-to-one correspondences

Children must learn to count objects by making one-to-one (1-1) counting correspondences so that each object is paired with exactly one number word. This task is more complex than it appears to adults, who are expert counters. The counting words are said over *time*, but the objects exist in *space*. The counter must link each word said *in time* to one object *in space*, usually by touching or pointing to each object as each word is said. This counting action requires two kinds of correct matches (1-to-1 correspondences):

- the matching in a moment of *time* when the action occurs and a word is said, and

- the matching in *space* where the counting action points to an object once and only once.

Children initially make errors in both of these kinds of correspondences.

Helping Children Learn the Number-Word List

Parents can say and then listen to the number list in the car, when waiting or walking somewhere, walking up or down stairs, while cooking, and at other times. Teachers and caregivers can lead a group or the whole class of children in saying the number list when they are waiting in line or at the table before snack or walking outdoors.

Individual children can be asked to count in a small group or while others are playing outdoors or at other moments to find out that child's current number list. The teacher can then work briefly with the child on the words that are just beyond their last correct word.

For example, if the child counted "One, two, three, nine, ten, one, three," the teacher might say, "Four comes after three. Listen: One two three *four*. Say it with me: One two three *four*. Now you try it." The teacher helps with *four* as needed and goes on to add *five* after *four* if the child does four easily. Some children are helped by a rhythm in the count: "One, two, three; four, five, six."

- The word and point may not match in time. A child—

    a) may point at an object but not say a word, or

    b) may point at an object and say two or more words.

- The point may not match the objects in space. A child—

    a) may point at the same object more than once, or

    b) may skip an object.

These errors in space are usually more frequent than the errors in time. Skipping objects is especially frequent, especially for larger sets.

Four factors strongly affect the accuracy of counting correspondence:

- the amount of counting experience (more experience leads to fewer errors),

- the size of the set (children become accurate on small sets first),

- the arrangement of objects (objects in a row make it easier to keep track of what has been counted and what has not), and

- effort.

Parents and teachers need to model correct counting of small sets. They can hold the child's hand and help the child feel accurate counting. It is also helpful for adults or older siblings or children in a class to describe how to count, for example:

- Remember that each object needs one point and one number word, and you can't skip any.

- Remember where you started in the circle so that you stop just before that.

But children will continue to make counting errors even when they understand the task, because counting is a complex activity. After a parent or teacher is sure that a child understands correct counting, it is not necessary to correct every error. Saying "Try hard" or "Slow down" can help children concentrate and be correct.

Written number symbols

Children learn written number symbols through having such symbols around them named by their number word (e.g., "That's a two"). Parents and teachers vary in how much they do this naming, so children vary also. Unlike much of the number core that has been discussed, learning these word-visual pairs is mostly rote learning. But parts of particular numbers, or an overall impression (e.g., 1 is just a stick), can be elicited and discussed. Learning to recognize the numerals is not a difficult task. Some two- and three-year-olds have learned to read some numerals at home. Given experiences where they see the numeral and say its number word, early 2s/3s can learn several written number symbols.

The Number Core: Later 2s/3s

Overview

Children can take a crucial step during this period: They can coordinate counting and seeing cardinality to understand that the last word they say when they count tells how many there are (tells the cardinality). They begin to see numbers hiding inside small numbers (e.g., "I see one and two in the three cups"). They can say the number word list to ten. Their counting becomes more accurate, with frequent correct counts of groups up to five or six. With experience, they can read the written number symbols 1 through 5.

Coordinating the components of the number core

The last word said in counting a group of things tells *how many* are in that group. This idea involves a count-to-cardinal shift in word meaning. When counting, one must at the end of the counting action make a mental shift—

- from thinking of the last counted word as referring to *the last* counted *thing* (when pointing to the last cup)

- to thinking of that word as referring to *all the things* (the number of things in the whole set, i.e., the *cardinality* of the group).

For example, when counting five plates on the table as one, two, three, four, five, the *five* refers to the single last plate pointed to when saying "five." But then the counter must shift to thinking of all of the plates and think of the "five" as meaning all of them: "There are five plates on the table." This is a major conceptual milestone for young children (see fig. 2.1). Adults and even older children make that shift so quickly and automatically that we do not even know we are doing it.

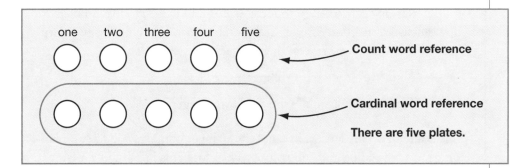

Fig. 2.1. Relating counting and cardinality

When children discover this relationship, they tend to apply it to all counts no matter the size of the set of objects. Therefore, children immediately generalize and apply this type of principle learning fairly consistently. It is relatively easy to teach children this relationship. For example, a statement of this principle followed by three demonstrations followed by another statement of the principle (see sidebar "Teaching the Cardinality Principle") was sufficient to move twenty of twenty-two children aged two years eight months to three years eleven months to using the principle (Fuson 1988).

Before children learn this relationship, they may count each time you ask "How many?" To them, "How many?" is a request to count, not a request for a cardinality. Or children may have a favorite cardinality that they say at the end of each count if asked how many, as this mother recorded in her notes about her daughter aged two years seven months:

Putting prunes back into a box, you correctly counted them up to nine. When asked how many prunes, you said *three* (your standard how many answer at this point: *three eyes*, etc.).

Even after being able to give the last counted word as the answer to "How many?" some children initially understand only that this last word answers the "How many?" question. They do not fully grasp the more abstract idea of cardinality as referring to all the objects. Thus, they may not point to all the objects when asked the cardinality question "Show me the four cups." Instead, they may point at the last cup again. It is important to note that responding with the last word is progress. As children work more with this relationship, and with activities discussed in the relations and operations sections, they will work out the relationship between counting and cardinality more fully. Parents and teachers can show the meaning of "Show me the four cups" by gesturing around or across all four cups. But if the child does not get this cardinal idea after a couple of examples, drop it and try again at a later time when the child may be more able to take this conceptual step.

Extending cardinality

Numbers on fingers

Later 2s/3s begin to learn to recognize and to make groups of fingers that show small cardinalities. This ability often begins when their family shows them how to show their age on their fingers:

- "I am two" (showing two fingers), or
- "I am three years old" (showing three fingers).

This is an important process because these finger numbers will later on become tools for adding and subtracting. Therefore, it is important for later 2s/3s to work on showing fingers for one, two, three, four, and five without counting them out. Of course, initially they will need to raise a finger with each new count word to find out which fingers show a given number.

Cultures vary in how they show numbers on fingers. The three major ways are to—

- start with the thumb and move across the hand to the little finger;
- start with the little finger and move across the hand to the thumb;

- start with the pointing finger, move across to the little finger, and then raise the thumb.

Some cultures raise all the fingers and then lower them as they count (e.g., this is frequently done in Japan). But most cultures start with the hand closed and raise fingers with each count word. Some cultures show numbers one way for age and another for counting when adding, and so on. Teachers should find out how children in their class show numbers on their fingers and support that method. In classrooms where children use different methods, many children become fluent in showing numbers in different ways.

Partners hiding inside other numbers

Later 2s/3s begin to see and say the small numbers 1, 2, 3 inside other numbers if they have been given opportunities to hear and say such language. This example occurred at home after a child heard similar sentences on *Sesame Street* where pictures were shown with the sentence: The child asked for four olives, and her father gave them to her. She said, "Two and two make four."

This process is often called *conceptual subitizing* (Clements 1999) because it involves seeing the small numbers rather than counting them. Calling these smaller numbers *partners* helps children relate these two smaller numbers within the total. For example, *one* and *two* are *partners* of *three*. With experience, children move rapidly from the partners to revisualizing them to see the total and can even express this relationship in words, as in the foregoing example. Children need opportunities to see and hear such partner sentences at home and at care or educational centers. Other examples are given in "Activities for Number Partners Hiding Inside Other Numbers" on the next page. These issues will be discussed more in the section on operations.

Extending the number-word list

If children have opportunities to hear the number-word list beyond their accurate range, they will extend this accurate portion of their list. With such experiences, later 2s/3s can count to ten and are working on the irregular teen patterns and the twenty to twenty-nine pattern.

Extending counting accuracy

Later 2s/3s continue to generalize what they can count and extend their accurate counting to larger sets. Children with little experience with books may have more difficulty counting pictures of objects rather than objects themselves. Therefore, it is important that all children practice counting pictures of objects as well as objects.

Very young children counting small rows with high effort make more errors in which their say-point *actions do not correspond in time* than errors in the

Activities for Number Partners Hiding Inside Other Numbers

1)   Adult: "How many balls?"

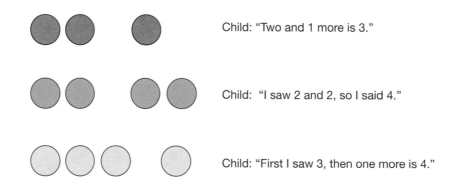

Child: "Two and 1 more is 3."

Child: "I saw 2 and 2, so I said 4."

Child: "First I saw 3, then one more is 4."

2)   Have the child make number partner displays (like in 1 above) for an adult or another child.

Matteo: Becky: "3 and 2 more is 5."

3)   Have children look for number partners hiding inside other numbers in pictures in books.

4)   For children who are already good at the previous activities, do a "snapshots" version of activity (1). Hide a small number of objects in your hands. Tell children they should take a snapshot picture in their mind when you open your hands. Open your hands briefly to show the objects. Then close your hands and ask how many objects there were in all. Allow more viewing time if needed.

spatial matching of the points and objects. Thus, they may need more practice coordinating their actions of saying one word and pointing at an object. Energetic collective practice in which children rhythmically say the number-word list and move their hand down with a finger pointed out as each word is said can be helpful. To vary the practice, the words can sometimes be said loudly and sometimes softly, but always with emphasis (a regular beat). The points can involve a large motion of the whole arm or a smaller motion, but again in a regular beat with each word. Coordinating these actions of saying and pointing is the goal for overcoming this type of error. For variety, these activities can involve other movements, such as marching around the room with rhythmic arm motions or stamping a foot, saying a count word each time. See "Examples of Incomplete Understanding of Counting" on the next page.

Young children sometimes make multiple count errors on the last object. They either find it difficult to stop, or they think they need to say a certain number of words when counting and just keep on counting so they say that many. When they say the number-word list, more words *are* better. They need to learn that saying the number-word list when counting objects is controlled by the number of objects. Reminding them that even the last object gets only one word and one point can help. They also may need the physical support of holding their hand as they reach to point to the last object so that the hand can be stopped from extra points. When doing this, say the last word loudly and stretched out (e.g., "fii-i-i-ve") to help the child inhibit saying the next word.

Regularity and rhythmicity are important aspects of counting. Activities that increase these aspects can be helpful to children making lots of correspondence errors. Children who are not discouraged about their counting competence generally enjoy counting all sorts of things and will do so if there are objects they can count at home or in a care or educational center. Counting in pairs of children to check each other so as to find and correct errors is often fun for the pairs. Counting within other activities, such as building towers with blocks, should also be encouraged.

Extending written number symbols

If children have opportunities to see a written number symbol and hear its number word, they will extend the number of symbols they know. With such experiences, later two- and three-year-olds can recognize and say the number words for 1, 2, 3, 4, 5 and perhaps other numerals.

Coordinating count words, quantities, and written numerals

Two- and three-year-olds are working on all six of the relationships shown by the three line segments in figure 2.2 on page 21 (each relationship goes both ways). Quantities as seen or as counted cardinalities, count words, and written numerals become connected and form the foundation for later work with these numbers in relations and operations.

Monitoring and Correcting Children's Count Errors

Parents and teachers do not have to monitor or correct children's counting all the time. It is much more important for all children to get frequent counting practice, want to count and feel confident about it, and watch and help one another. Once children basically understand correct counting, they still will continue to make some errors, especially with larger sets. Children who do not show some correspondence between count words, points, and objects do need help until they can do so. Sometimes the adult can do part of the activity, such as the pointing, and can support the child by counting along. Some children need the adult to hold their pointing hand to get the motor feedback about what correct counting is. But for those who basically understand, frequent reminders to the whole class (or by a parent hearing or seeing a count error from afar) about the general process can be helpful:

- Remember not to skip over any.
- Remember to point one time to each thing.
- Try hard! You can do it!

Effort is a big part of correct counting. Children who make the same particular count errors do need support to overcome those errors through modeling by the adult or being helped physically with the pointing and counting. Establishing an exaggerated rhythm can help make correspondences; the child can back down to a more relaxed counting when the correspondences are going well.

Examples of Incomplete Understanding of Counting

Child 1: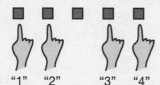

Child 2: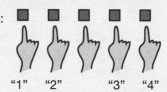

Child 3: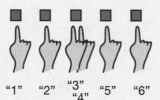

Child 4: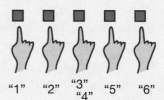

Child 5: Keeps counting past 5.

Child 6: Doesn't know that the last number word said tells how many objects there are, so counts over again when asked "How many in all?"

Activities for Children to Practice

1) Rhythmic counting with hops (or claps, arm movements, and so on):

"We hopped _____ (or five) times!"

2) Counting wand: rhythmically count together while the teacher (or later, a child) points to children (or objects) one by one.

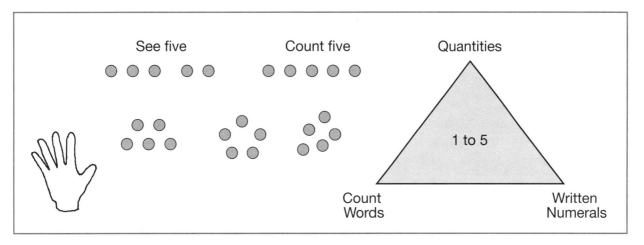

Fig. 2.2. Relate quantities, count words, and written number symbols

The Number Core: 4s/Pre-Ks

Overview

Children at this level make another major conceptual advance: They can shift from a *cardinal* meaning of a number to its *counting* meaning and *remember that number* as they count out objects. So they can successfully do such things as follow the direction "Put five napkins on the table." In the other number core areas, 4s/pre-Ks who have had opportunities at home or in a care or educational center to learn the number-core content outlined in the foregoing for 2s/3s extend their competencies to larger numbers. Teachers or caregivers who must support a mixture of some children who have learned the previous number-core content and those who have not had sufficient opportunity to learn can frequently combine these groups of children by allowing children to choose set sizes with which they feel comfortable and can succeed. Varied sizes of number can also be used at learning centers. Some children may need extra time and support tasks to extend their competence to larger numbers. It is crucial that they receive this support to compensate for lack of earlier learning opportunities.

Relating counting and cardinality

From the cardinal word to the count word: Count out n things

The major conceptual advance of being able to count out a given number of objects (e.g., six) requires a child to remember the number *six* while counting. This is more difficult for larger numbers because the child has to remember the number longer. Children initially trying to count out a given number of things often count past the number because their counting is not fluent enough to—

- count a long sequence of words,

Errors in Singular Count and Plural Cardinal Language

The cardinal reference to all the things in a group uses a number word and a plural noun: "Those are the five chips." The count reference to any object where a particular count word was said uses a number word and a singular noun: "This is where I said 'five'" (pointing to the last chip). Children initially may reverse this singular/plural language, as in the following examples of responses to the cardinality-reference question "Are these the *n* soldiers (chips)?"

- "Those are five soldiers," said as the child points to the last soldier. [cardinal language *five soldiers* but count reference to one last object]

- "This one's the five chips," said as the child points to the last chip. [cardinal language *five chips* but count reference to one last object]

- "This is the six soldiers," said as the child points to each soldier (said six times). [cardinal language *six soldiers* but count reference to one object, although saying and pointing in succession to each object is a form of cardinality]

- "This is the four chips," said as the child points to the last chip. [cardinal language *four chips* but count reference to one last object]

- "This is where I said chip four," said as the child's hands gesture to all the chips. [count language *chip*

(Continued on page 24)

- remember a number, and

- monitor with each count whether they have reached the number yet.

This difficulty emphasizes how much children need to practice counting things. It is not enough to be accurate. Counting needs to be so easy for the child that she or he has enough extra thinking capacity to remember the number to which she or he is counting.

Counting out a specified number is needed for solving addition and subtraction problems and for doing various real-life tasks, so this is an important milestone. Children can practice this milestone by counting out *n* things for various family and school purposes. Such practice can also occur in gamelike activities in which someone can help remember the number. Children who are struggling with this task, even for small numbers, need more practice just in basic counting of things so that they become fast and confident.

The conceptual advance for counting out *n* things is the reverse of learning that the last count word tells how many there are (the *count-to-cardinal* shift). To count out six things, a child is being told how many there are (a *cardinal* meaning) and must then shift to a *count* meaning of that six, that is, listen to and monitor the count words as they are said ("Have I said 'six' yet?") to stop when they say the counting word *six*. They must make a cardinal-to-count shift.

Verbal knowledge of singulars and plurals for cardinal and counting references continues to be learned by 4s/pre-Ks. Even children who gesture correctly to show their count meaning (*gesture to one thing*) or their cardinal meaning (*gesture to the whole set*) may struggle with correct verbal expressions. Children initially may make the kinds of errors shown in the sidebar "Errors in Singular Count and Plural Cardinal Language."

Relating quantities, count words, and written number symbols

4s/pre-Ks extend the triad relationships that 2s/3s had made between all pairs in the triad of quantities, count words, and written number symbols for the numbers 1 to 5 (see fig. 2.3). Four-year-olds/prekindergartners can work on seeing and making 5-groups in fingers and with objects and drawings, as discussed in the next section. Some ways to do so are shown at the top right of figure 2.3 for eight. Five fingers (one hand) and three fingers show eight. The other three visual models also show a group of five and a group of three arranged under or beside the 5 so that children can see the relationship. The important thing is that the five things be easily perceived as a separate group. Children with experience also can make the triad relationships shown in figure 2.3 for other seen and counted cardinalities for all numbers 1 to 10. The cards shown at the bottom right of figure 2.3 are an easy way to help children practice the triad relationships for numbers 1 to 5 and for the 5-groups for numbers 6 to 10. They can say the count word for either side, and they can match two cards using two sets of cards 5 to 10.

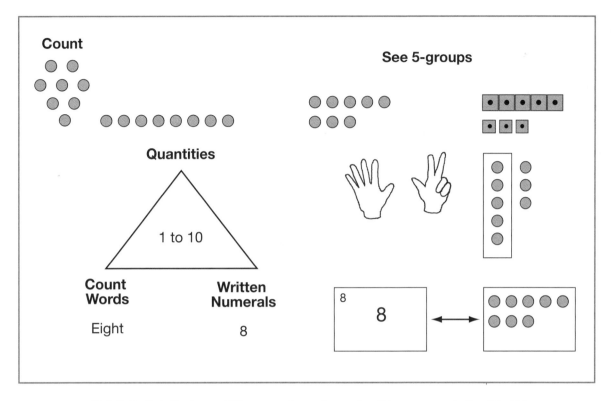

Fig. 2.3. Relating quantities, count words, and written numerals for 1 to 10

Cardinality

Children extend the numbers for which they can see partners hiding inside. For example, children might say "I see one thumb and four fingers make my five fingers." The 5-groups are particularly important and useful both now and later in the learning path. These 5-groups offer a good way to understand the numbers 6, 7, 8, 9, 10 as 5 + 1, 5 + 2, 5 + 3, 5 + 4, 5 + 5 (see fig. 2.4 on page 25). The convenient relationship to fingers (5 on one hand) provides a kinesthetic component as well as a visual aspect to this knowledge. Without focused experience with 5-groups, children's notions of the numbers 6 through 10 tend to be hazy beyond a general sense that the numbers are getting larger. Figure 2.4 shows at the top a display that might be made large and posted in a room and might also be put on a worksheet to be sure that all children can see it. Children would discuss patterns they see in the 5-groups, and discuss relationships with the circle 5-groups and the 5-groups in their fingers. Part C on page 26 shows a worksheet that could be mathematized in a discussion to find the 5-groups in this park situation. Children could then find and make 5-groups with objects in their classroom. Things in the real world are often actually arranged and sold in groups of five and ten in many other countries of the world, but rarely here. So children need to see examples nicely organized and with simple pictures so that the patterns are easy to see. Seeing the 5-groups in the simplest form, just with circles, is particularly helpful. Part B of figure 2.4 shows a worksheet example that is a follow-up *four* but cardinal gesture reference to all of the chips]

Children can overcome these errors with modeling and practice. A teacher or parent can give general statements along with modeling correct language. The following are examples:

· "When we tell how many there are in all, we move our hand around all the blocks like this" [point in an ellipse around the objects or move an open hand back and forth across the objects]. "And we say how many like this: 'These are seven blocksssss.' Now let's do it together. Show me with your hand and say how many." [Gesture and say, "These are seven blocksssss" with the children.] "Now you do it without me." This can be repeated until children can say the statement alone. Of course children may need more opportunities to hear and say it correctly.

practice activity after experience with objects; it supports matching by drawing lines to make the matches and allows individual practice. This page also can then be discussed by children to help them articulate relationships between the 5-groups in the fingers and in the circle format.

Knowing the 5-groups is helpful at the next level in kindergarten as children add and subtract numbers with totals of 6 through 10. The patterns are problem-solving tools that can be drawn or used mentally. Children in East Asia learn and use these 5-group patterns throughout their early numerical learning. In grade 1 they use the 5-groups to support their mental methods for adding and subtracting with teen totals by making a ten (see table 2.2 discussed in the operations core). Using 5-groups or other partners of numbers is part of the relations/operations core and is discussed more there.

Children can be helped to see partners hiding inside a number by using simple objects or pictures. The partners can be shown by color, by circling the groups, or as two groups of things close to each other or in a pattern. Objects showing a number can be moved apart to show partners hiding inside that number. Worksheets can also stimulate finding and discussing partners. The partners in part C of figure 2.4 can be identified and discussed: for example, the four dogs are made by two dogs and two dogs, and the five people are composed of four children and one grown-up.

Number-word list
Number words from eleven to nineteen

The first ten number words are arbitrary in most languages. But then most languages begin to have patterns that make them easier to learn. English has a partial pattern for words from eleven to nineteen, but this pattern is marred by irregularities. For simplicity we call these numbers *teen* numbers even though not all number words for these numbers have the -*teen* suffix.

- The partial pattern is to say a word for a number below ten and add -*teen* to it (the -*teen* means *ten*), as in *sixteen, seventeen, eighteen, nineteen*.

- However, the first two "teen" words (*eleven, twelve*) do not have the -*teen* ending.

- The third and fifth words have modified the number below ten so that it may not be recognizable: *thirteen* instead of *threeteen* and *fifteen* instead of *five teen*.

Children frequently see and use the -*teen* structure before they learn the exceptions, as in this diary example for a child aged three years two months: "Eight, nine, ten, eleventeen, twelveteen, thirteen." Parents and teachers can discuss these irregularities, for example:

- "What would be better number words than eleven and twelve?" (oneteen and twoteen).

- "What would be clearer to say than fifteen?" (fiveteen)

• "Yes, it is harder to have some of the number words we have. But we need to use them or other people will not understand us."

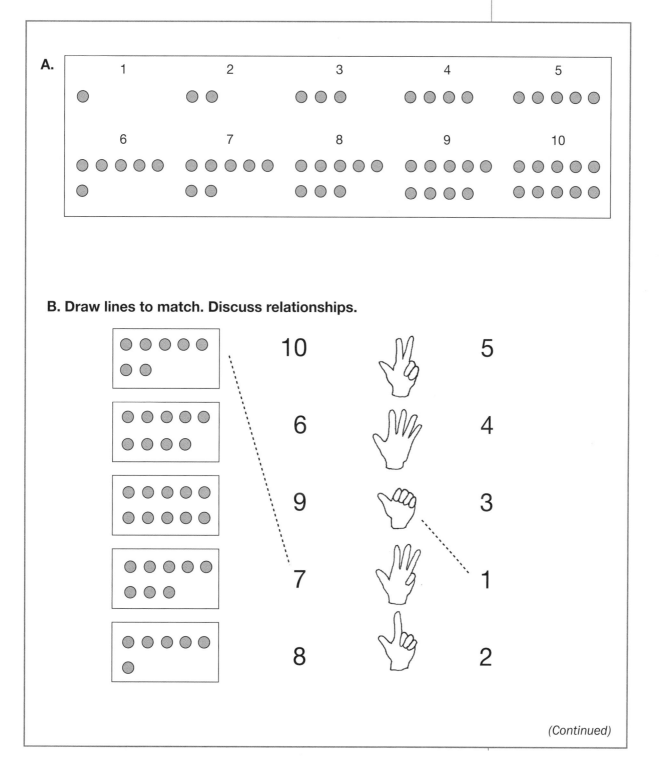

B. Draw lines to match. Discuss relationships.

(Continued)

Fig. 2.4. Seeing 5-groups that show 6 as 5 + 1, 7 as 5 + 2, 8 as 5 + 3, 9 as 5 + 4, and 10 as 5 + 5

C.

Fig. 2.4.—*Continued*

Many children skip over fifteen even when they can say the end of the teens ("sixteen, seventeen, eighteen, nineteen") correctly. This may be because it is in the middle and because it is irregular. So parents and teachers may need to work particularly on the word *fifteen*.

This *ones-before-tens* structure of the teen words is opposite to the *tens-before-ones* structure in the written teen number symbols. We say *four* first in *fourteen* but write 4 second in 14 (1 ten 4 ones). This reversal, and the irregularities listed in the foregoing, make the pattern-finding activity of relating written numerals to teen number words particularly complex for children speaking English. They need help and support to learn to say the teen numbers correctly.

A final difficulty in understanding the meaning of the teens words is that English words do not explicitly say the *ten* that is in the teen number (*teen* does not mean *ten* even to many adults). This is in contrast with number words in East Asia that are said "ten, ten one, ten two, ten three," and so on, for 10, 11, 12, 13, and so on. Therefore, English-speaking children need particular help with visual cardinalities that show the ten inside teen numbers. This is a goal for kindergarten and is discussed more fully in *Focus in Kindergarten* (NCTM, forthcoming). It is important for all 4s/pre-Ks to be able to say the number-word list to twenty even if they do not yet understand the ten within each teen number. Advanced 4s/pre-Ks can count out a group of teen objects (for example, 16) and then pull apart ten to show the 1 ten hiding inside sixteen. These ten objects can be in a group or arranged in a column to the left of the 6 ones. This arrangement makes the objects look like the numeral 16.

Number words from twenty to ninety-nine

The *ones-before-tens* structure for English teen numbers comes from German. The same structure is used in German for all numbers from eleven to ninety-nine. But English changes for the words from twenty to ninety-nine to the reverse *tens-before-ones* structure. This is the same order in which numerals are written: *twenty* is said first in *twenty-seven* and 2 is written first in 27 (2 tens 7 ones). So it is easier for children to relate the patterns in the written numerals to English number words from twenty to ninety-nine, a goal for kindergarten. Fuller understanding of the quantities of tens and ones in these numbers is a goal for grade 1. But 4s/pre-Ks can begin the process of learning the cyclic pattern in the number-word list for twenty, twenty-one, twenty-two, twenty-three, …, twenty-nine and also for thirty to thirty-nine. Children can begin to learn this second pattern even while they are working on the teen pattern. A diary entry made at the same time as the foregoing eleventeen, twelveteen, thirteen example says, "You were standing alone and raising the correct number of ones fingers and concentrating very hard: *twenty-one, twenty-two, twenty-three, twenty-four, twenty-five.* Each *twen* was very long. You count everything. You love to count."

The transition from nine to ten is not clear: *ten* just sounds like another counting word (nine, ten, eleven, …) with no special significance. Saying "one-ten zero-ones" would tell the meaning of this word. Because young children do not yet understand this quantity meaning as one group of ten, at first children often do not stop at *twenty-nine* but continue to count, "twenty-nine, twenty-ten, twenty-eleven, twenty-twelve, twenty-thirteen." This error can be a mixture of not yet understanding that the pattern ends at nine and difficulty stopping the usual counting at nine so as to shift to another decade.

With practice and support, 4s/pre-Ks can learn to count to thirty-nine, and they are working on the correct order of the decades to one hundred. Saying the number-word list correctly to one hundred is a kindergarten goal, but advanced 4s/pre-Ks may accomplish it. Again, irregularities in English decade number words complicate this task. *Forty, sixty, seventy, eighty, ninety* have a regular pattern: the ones word followed by *-ty* (which means ten). But most of the early decade words are irregular:

- *Twenty (two-tens)*, not *twoty*

- *Thirty (three-tens)*, not *threety*

- *Fifty (five tens)*, not *fivety*

As with the teen words, the *ten* is not said explicitly but is said as a different suffix *-ty*. Therefore, as discussed in *Focus in Grade 1* (NCTM, forthcoming), children need to work explicitly with groups of tens and ones to understand these meanings for the number words from twenty to one hundred.

Children can learn and practice the number-word list by hearing and by saying it without doing anything else, or it can be heard or said in coordination with an action like jumping or climbing stairs. Saying it alone allows the child to concentrate on the word, and on the patterns in the words. Parents and teachers can discuss the patterns with children. They can also help children with the transitions: *twenty-nine, thirty* and *thirty-nine, forty*. Accuracy in saying the number-word list is not enough. The list has to be very fluent so that it can be used for counting objects.

Structured learning experiences decrease the time it takes to learn the pattern of decades to one hundred (ten, twenty, thirty, forty, … ninety) and help children learn to use this decade list with the *n-ty to n-ty-nine* pattern. Without the good start as 4s/pre-Ks in learning teens and the early decades twenty to twenty-nine and thirty to thirty-nine, too many children at present fail to become fluent in the count to one hundred at kindergarten. Even some students enter grade 2 without this fluency. This fluency is important for understanding and then using the tens and ones quantities in grade 1 and grade 2. Four-year-olds/prekindergartners enjoy learning and saying the patterns in twenty to twenty-nine and thirty to thirty-nine.

Counting correspondences

Four-year-olds/prekindergartners can extend considerably the set size they are able to count accurately. For objects in a row or objects they can move, most 4s/pre-Ks can count with only occasional errors even with large sets of fifteen and above. As before, effort continues to be important. Children who are tired or discouraged may make many more errors than they make after a simple prompt to "try hard" or "count slowly."

On larger sets, 4s/pre-Ks occasionally make point-object errors in which an object is skipped or pointed to more than once. These errors seem to stem from momentary lack of attention rather than lack of coordination. If children are skipping over many objects, they need to be asked to "count carefully and don't skip any." Trying hard or counting slowly can also reduce these errors.

When two counts of the same set disagree, many children of this age think that their second count is correct and so do not count again. Calling attention to the inconsistency and helping them value the strategy of counting a third time can increase the accuracy of their counts.

Accurate counting depends on three things:

a) knowing the patterns in the number-word list so that a correct number-word list can be said,

b) correctly assigning one number word to one object (1-1 correspondence), and

c) keeping track of which objects have already been counted so that they are not counted more than once.

Keeping track—differentiating counted from uncounted entities—is most easily done by moving objects into a counted set. Doing so is not possible with things that cannot be moved, such as pictures in a book. Strategies for keeping track of messy, large sets continue to develop for many years, and even adults are not entirely accurate.

Written number symbols

4s/pre-Ks continue to extend the written number symbols that they can read and can learn to read the numerals 1, 2, 3, 4, 5, 6, 7, 8, 9, and 10. Children at this level can begin to write some numerals, often beginning with the easier numerals 1, 3, and 7.

The Relations (More Than/Less Than) Core

Overview

The relations core goals require children to learn to perceive, say, discuss, and create the relations *more than, less than,* and *equal to* on two sets. Initially 2s/3s use general perceptual, length, or density strategies to decide whether one set is more than, less than, or equal to another set. Gradually these are replaced by more accurate strategies. To decide which is more, 4s/pre-Ks can match the entities in the sets to find out which has leftover entities, or they can count both sets and use understandings of more than/less than order relations on numbers. Eventually in grade 1, children begin to see the third set potentially present in relational situations, the *difference* between the smaller

---

Correcting Children's Counting Errors

As long as children *understand* that correct counting requires one point and one word for each object and are trying to do that, parents and teachers do not need to correct errors all the time. As with many physical activities, counting will improve with practice and does not need to be perfect each time. It is much more important for all children to get frequent counting practice and watch and help each other, with occasional help and corrections from the teacher. Of course, children struggling to make correspondences can be helped as suggested in the foregoing for younger children.

and the larger set. In this way, relational situations become the third kind of addition/subtraction situation, *additive comparison,* discussed in the operations core for grades 1 and 2.

The relations core: 2s/3s

Relations: more than, equal to, less than

Two- and three-year-olds begin to learn the language involved in relations. *More* is a word learned by many children before they are two. Initially it is an action directive that means "Give me more of this." But gradually children become able to see cardinalities (use perceptual subitizing) and use length or density strategies to judge which of two sets has more things, for example, "She has more than I have because her row of blocks goes out here" (length) or "These are close together" (density). Such comparisons may not be correct at this age level if the sets are larger than three because children focus on length or on density and cannot yet coordinate these dimensions or effectively use the strategies of matching or counting.

Children also hear and therefore say the word *more* much more often than they hear or say *less.* Some children initially think that *less* means *more* because they think of the relationship in only one direction (they usually want more of something, so this focus makes sense). Thus it is important for children to hear both words even though they might not start using *less* until they are at the 4s/pre-Ks level.

English has the difficult distinction between *fewer* for objects that one counts and *less* for continuous quantities and numerals. This distinction is not important in prekindergarten, kindergarten, and primary school. Using and coming to understand the words *more* and *less* is sufficient throughout primary school.

Two- and three-year-olds can begin to use the words *more* and *less* with specific very small numbers of things. For example:

- One is less than two.

- Three is more than two.

The relations core: 4s/pre-Ks

Relations: more than, equal to, less than

Four-year-olds/prekindergartners continue to use the perceptual strategies they used earlier (general perceptual, length, density). But they can also begin to use matching and counting to find which is less and which is more. However, they can also be easily misled by perceptual cues. For example, the classic task used by Piaget (1941/1965) involved two rows of aligned objects. Then the objects in one row were moved apart so one row was longer (or occasionally, moved together so one row was shorter). The top row of figure 2.5 shows the rows after one has been made longer. Many children aged four and five would say that the longer row has more. These children focused either on length or on density, but could not notice and coordinate both. However, when asked to count in such situations, many four-year-olds can count both rows accurately, remember both count words, and decide that the two rows have the same number. Thus, many 4s/pre-Ks may need encouragement to count in more-than/less-than/equal-to situations and especially when the perceptual information is misleading. But they can learn to use their counting information correctly, as shown in figure 2.5.

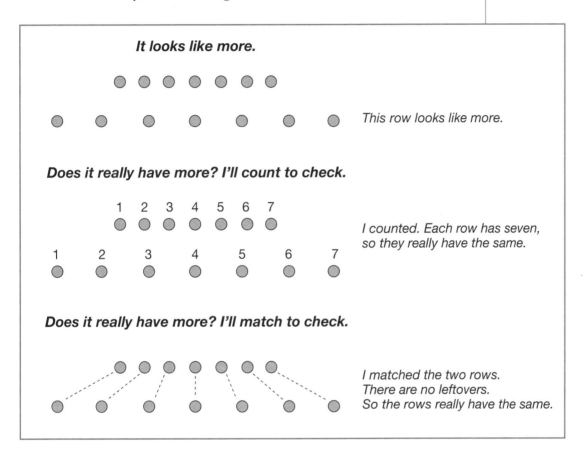

Fig. 2.5. Does it look like more or really have more?

When children are using perceptual strategies and also beginning to count to find which set has more or less, they may say such sentences as "This *seven* has more than this *seven*." Such children are confusing two meanings of *more:*

- looks like more, and

- really has more.

They need help differentiating these two different meanings (see fig. 2.5). The teacher or more advanced children can model this difference in meanings by asking,

- "Which looks like it has more?" and

- "Does it really have more?"

They might also share their own thoughts by "thinking aloud":

> "This seven looks like more to me because there are things that stick out here, but they must have the same amount because I counted them and they both have seven."

Counting again to check your counting can also be modeled:

> "Oh, I wonder if I counted wrong. I'm going to count very carefully this time and count them both again. I might even need to count a third time to check myself."

A parent or teacher might also suggest matching as another way to check whether they have the same and show how this is done if no one can do it correctly. Such matching is often easiest in drawings where the matching lines are actually drawn. See examples of matching by moving objects and by drawing lines in the "Comparing Activity" on the next page.

To use counting to decide *more/less*, children need to be able to count both sets accurately and remember the first count result while counting the second set. Herein is another example of the need for fluency in counting. Without such fluency, some children forget their first count result by the time they have counted the second set. These children need more counting practice. Children also need to know order relations on cardinal numbers. They need to learn the general pattern that most children do derive from the order of the counting words: the number that tells *more* is farther along (said later) in the number-word list than is the number that tells *less*. Discussions in which children make sets for both numbers in rows, match them and count them, and discuss the results can help them establish this general pattern.

To use matching successfully to find more than/less than, children may need to learn how to match by making line segments with their finger or their eyes to connect pairs. They can draw such matching lines if the compared sets are drawn on paper. Then they need to know that the number with any extra objects is more than the other set. It is also helpful to match using actual objects, moving the objects so that they are aligned. Here it is also important to keep the two compared groups visually separate.

Before research on counting and matching was done, some researchers and early childhood educators suggested that teachers should not do any number activities, such as adding and subtracting, until after children could do the Piagetian conservation of number task: that is, could know and say that rows in the Piagetian task at the top of figure 2.5 were equal even in the face of misleading perceptual transformations like making one row longer. However, now we know that four- and five-year-olds go through a crucial stage in which using counting and matching are important to learn and can lead to correct relational judgments (see research summarized in Clements and Sarama [2007, 2008]; Fuson [1992a, 1992b]). It is important and developmentally appropriate for children of this age to have experiences counting and matching to find *more, less,* or *equal.*

The Logical Necessity of Piagetian Conservation

It is true that children typically do not understand that the rows are equal out of a logical necessity until age 6 or 7 (sometimes not until age 8). These older children judge the rows to be equal on the basis of mental transformations that they apply to the situation. They do not need to count or match after one row is made shorter or longer by moving objects in it together or apart to see that they are equal. They are certain that simply moving the objects in the set does not change the numerosity. This is what Piaget meant by conservation of number. But children can work effectively with situations involving *more* and *less* years before they have this advanced meaning of conservation of number.

Comparing Activity

Adult asks: "Are there enough bones for each dog to get one?"

(a) With objects that can be moved:

(b) With a drawing where the child can draw matching lines:

Possible **math talk** for either case:
Adult: "Are there more dogs or more bones?"
Katie: "More bones!"
Adult: "That's right, there are more bones. There are fewer dogs. How many more bones than dogs are there?"
Katie: "One more bone."

For progress in relations, it is important that 4s/pre-Ks hear, and try to use, the less common comparative terms *less, shorter, smaller* instead of only hearing or using *more, taller, bigger*. Teachers can also use the comparative terms (for example, *bigger* and *smaller* rather than just *big* and *small*) so that

Examples of Word-Problem Types

Each of these main types has an addition situation and a related subtraction situation.

Change-plus/change-minus situations:

Addition: change plus: "One bunny was in the garden. Two bunnies hopped into the garden. How many bunnies are in the garden now?"

Subtraction: change minus: "Four frogs were sitting on a log. Three frogs jumped off the log. How many frogs are on the log now?"

Put-together/take-apart situations:

Addition: put together: "Grammy has one red flower and two blue flowers. How many flowers does she have in all?"

Subtraction (unknown addend): take apart: "Mom bought three apples. One apple is red. The other apples are yellow. How many yellow apples are there?"

children gain experience with these forms, although not all children may become fluent in their use at this level.

The Operations (Addition and Subtraction) Core

Overview

In the operations core children learn to see addition and subtraction situations in the real world by focusing on the mathematical aspects of those situations and making a model of the situation: They *mathematize* these situations by focusing on the mathematical aspects of the situation (see the introduction for a discussion of *mathematizing*). Initially such mathematizing involves focusing on the *number of objects* rather than on their color, their size, or their use (e.g., "I see *two* red spoons and *one* blue spoon") and using those same objects to find the answer by *refocusing on the total* and seeing or counting it (e.g., "I see *three* spoons in all").

Types of addition/subtraction situations

Before kindergarten, children solve two types of addition/subtraction situations: change-plus/change-minus and put-together/take-apart.

Change-plus/change-minus situations have—

- an initial amount (the start),

- then some quantity is added to or taken from that amount (the change),

- creating the final amount (the result).

Put-together/take-apart (sometimes called *combine*) situations involve—

- two initial quantities that are put together to make a third quantity (put together), or

- one quantity that is taken apart to make two quantities (take apart).

In story problems at this age, the final amount is the focus of the question in the problem (see sidebar "Examples of Word-Problem Types"). In grade 1, the start quantity and the change quantity can be the unknown number, the focus of the question.

Language learning

Addition and subtraction situations, and the word problems that describe such situations, provide many wonderful opportunities for learning language. Word problems are short and fairly predictable texts. Children can vary the words in them while keeping much of the text. Children can say word problems in their own words and help everyone's understanding. English language learners can repeat such texts and vary particular words as they wish. All these learning activities require the support of visual objects or acted-out situations for children to learn the special mathematics vocabulary involved in addition and subtraction. Children should be encouraged to create their own word problems around their own situations both at home and in care or educational settings. These additive and subtractive learning situations provide wonderful opportunities for children to integrate art (drawing pictures), language practice, and pretend play.

Partners as embedded numbers

With experience in the foregoing addition/subtraction situations, children begin to learn to see partners (addends) hiding inside a number. Initially they see one such example. For example, children can take apart five to see that it can be made from a three and a two. Later on, they can take apart five things to see *all* its partners: three and two and also four and one. In kindergarten, these decomposed/composed numbers can be symbolized by such equations such as $5 = 3 + 2$ and $5 = 4 + 1$. Such equations give children experiences with the meaning of the = symbol as "is the same number as" and with algebraic equations with one number on the left. This is helpful in later algebra learning because many algebra students think that equations just produce an answer and that only one number can be alone on the right side of the equation.

Early in problem solving, children need to shift from seeing the total to seeing the partners (addends). With experience and fluency, they can simultaneously see the addend within the total or make the switch very rapidly. A young child watched her mother cut her peanut butter sandwich in half and those halves into halves and said, "Two and two make four."

We call this situation *embedded numbers:* the two partners (addends) are embedded within the total. Such embedded numbers, along with the number-word sequence skill of starting counting at any number, enable older children to move to the more advanced strategies described next.

Levels in addition/subtraction solution methods

A large body of research evidence describes the worldwide learning path of levels in addition and subtraction methods. Different methods can give the correct answer, and children can learn more by explaining and showing their own solution method. Teachers and parents can support children in such showing and explaining. The focus is less on the answer and much more on how the child thought about the problem. These levels are shown in table 2.2. Children before and in kindergarten are working at level 1. They use count-all strategies to solve addition problems and take-away strategies to solve subtraction problems. The conceptual embedded numbers described in the foregoing allow some kindergarten and all grade 1 children to move to a more advanced level of addition/subtraction solution procedures—level 2, counting on. Even later, children may move to level 3, recomposing methods.

Table 2.2
Levels of Children's Addition and Subtraction Methods

	8 + 6 = 14	14 − 8 = 6
Level 1: Count all	a 1 2 3 4 5 6 7 8 (○○○○○○○○) b 1 2 3 4 5 (○○○○○) 6 (○) c 1 2 3 4 5 (○○○○○) 6 7 8 (○○○) 9 10 11 12 13 (○○○○○) 14 (○)	a 1 2 3 4 5 6 7 8 9 10 11 12 13 14 (number line ○) b 1 2 3 4 5 6 7 8 (○○○○○○○○) 1 2 3 4 5 6 (○○○○○○) c
Level 2: Count on	8 (○○○○○○○○) 8 → 9 10 11 12 13 14 (○○○○○○) Or use fingers to keep track of the six counted on.	To solve 14 − 8: I count on 8 + ? = 14. 9 10 11 12 13 14 (fingers) I took away 8. 8 to 14 is 6, so 14 − 8 = 6.
Level 3: Recompose Make a 10 (general): one addend breaks apart to make 10 with the other addend.	10 + 4 (○○○○○○○○○○ ○○○○)	14 − 8: I make a 10 for 8 + ? = 14. (○○○○○○○○ ○○ ○○○○) 8 + 2 + 4 6 8 + 6 = 14
Make a 10 (from 5s within each addend).	6 + 8 = 6 + 6 + 2 = 12 + 2 = 14 (○○○○○○ + ○○○ ○○○○○)	
Doubles ± n		

Note: Many children attempt to count down for subtraction, but counting down is difficult and error-prone. Children are much more successful with counting on; it makes subtraction as easy as addition.

These will be discussed more fully in *Focus in Grade 1* (NCTM, forthcoming) and *Focus in Grade 2* (NCTM, forthcoming). The work on partners in pre-K and K develops vital prerequisites for these level 2 and level 3 methods.

Number core and operations core understandings outlined in this book are crucial for children to understand and gain fluency in level 1 methods. They also are the prerequisites for advancing to level 2 and then level 3 solution methods. To be successful in entering kindergarten, children need to learn as 2s/3s and 4s/pre-Ks to—

- be very fluent in counting,

- know which fingers show a number,

- know partners of numbers, and

- understand the level 1 addition/subtraction methods.

Visualizing numbers with 5-groups also is helpful in adding and subtracting and in learning the make-a-ten methods later on. The competencies listed above enable children to move readily on to building kindergarten understandings.

The operations core (addition and subtraction): 2s/3s

Two- and three-year-olds can solve change-plus/change-minus situations and put-together/take-apart situations with small numbers (totals ≤ 5) if the situation is presented with objects or if they are helped to use objects to model these situations. The actions in the situation are acted out with objects. For the adding situations,

- children see the first group and then the second group;

- then they must see all the objects together as the focus of the question, for example, "How many now?" or "How many flowers in all?"

If objects are not present, the child can be helped to count out objects for each of the first two sets and then count all the objects. For the subtracting situations,

- children see or make the initial total,

- then they take away or separate the known addend,

- then they focus on how many are left and see or count them.

Children can have experience in learning how to do such adding and subtracting from family members, in child care centers, and from media such as television and CDs. Children may subitize groups of one and two or count these or somewhat larger numbers. To find the total they may count or put together the subitized quantity into a pattern that is also just seen and not really counted (e.g., "Two and two make four"). Initially children may need to see the objects that are in the story, but soon they can imagine blocks or other counters to be those things in the story. See the examples in the sidebar "Subitizing: Seeing and Saying Partner Language for Situations."

The operations core (addition and subtraction): 4s/pre-Ks

Level 1 solution methods

For totals ≤ 8, 4s/pre-Ks use conceptual subitizing and cardinal counting to solve change-plus/change-minus and put-together/take-apart addition/subtraction situations. They also can solve story problems and oral number word problems (e.g., "How much is one and three?") without objects presenting the numbers initially. This requires children to count out a specified number of objects, which they begin to do at this level (see the foregoing discussion in the number core on counting out *n* objects).

Four-year-olds/prekindergartners become able to use their fingers to add or to subtract for totals ≤ 10. When counting all, they will—

- count out and raise fingers for the first addend,
- count out and raise fingers for the second addend, and
- then count all the raised fingers.

Some children learn at home or in a care center to put the addends on separate hands, while others continue on to the next fingers for the second addend (see sketch "Putting Addends on Separate Hands"). Using separate hands makes it easier to see the addends if both are ≤ 5. Children using the method of putting fingers on separate hands eventually can just raise the fingers for the addends without counting out the fingers. They still need initially to count the total, but later they might just recognize it by sight or by feel. Children continuing to the next fingers for the second addend learn to put up the first addend and recognize the total without counting, but they need to count the second addend. Children who put addends on separate hands may have difficulty with problems with addends over five (e.g., 6 + 3) because one cannot put both such numbers on a separate hand. They could, however, shift to the method of raising fingers from the first addend. Such problems with totals ≤ 8 will only involve adding 1 or 2; such continuations of one and two are relatively easy.

When subtracting on their fingers, children raise fingers to show the total and then bend down or separate the fingers that show the number taken away (the known addend). They then can see or count the remaining fingers to find what is left (the unknown addend).

Some people worry that children who use their fingers will end up using them "as a crutch" and will not advance. But the research-based methods shown in table 2.2 demonstrate that fingers are used in different ways. At level 1 they are used as the objects that present the situation and that are added or taken away. But at level 2, the number words themselves have become the

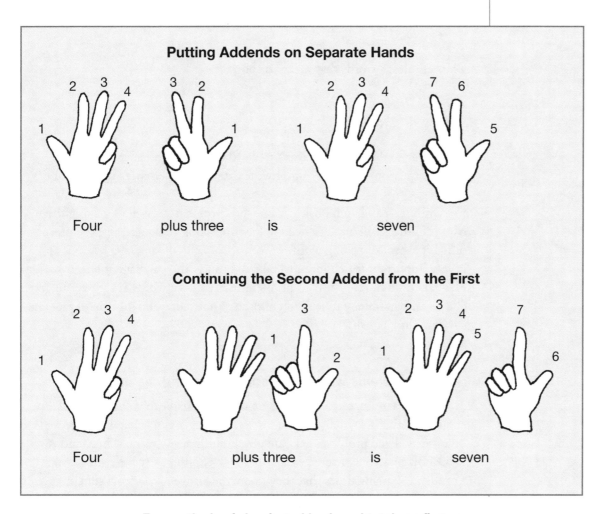

Putting Addends on Separate Hands

Four   plus three   is   seven

Continuing the Second Addend from the First

Four   plus three   is   seven

Two methods of showing addends and totals on fingers

objects that present the situation and that are added or taken away. The fingers count or match the second addend when counting on. For example, for 6 + 3, the child says "six" and puts up a successive finger with each number while counting on from 6: first finger with "seven," second finger with "eight," third finger with "nine." These level 2 methods are advanced enough to be used for life. So fingers are a learning tool used worldwide. The important consideration is that children in grade 1 advance on to using fingers in level 2 counting on and not remain at level 1 methods.

Language use

By experiences of relating actions and words in a story situation, children gradually extend their vocabulary of words that mean to add:

- *In all*

- *Put together*

- *Altogether*

- *Total*

They also learn words that mean to subtract:

- *Are left*

- *Take away*

Discussing and sharing solutions to word problems and enacting addition/subtraction situations can provide extended experiences for language learning.

Children can begin posing such word problems as well as solving them. Most children will initially need help with asking the questions, the most difficult aspect of posing word problems. As with all language learning, it is very important for children to talk and to use the language themselves. Having children retell a word problem in their own words is a powerful general teaching strategy to extend children's knowledge and give them practice speaking in English.

Solving problems without objects presenting the problem

Four-year-olds/prekindergartners who have had experience with adding and subtracting situations when they were younger can generalize to solve decontextualized problems that are posed numerically, as in "Three and two make how many?" For some small numbers, children may have solved such a problem so many times that they know the answer as a verbal statement: "Two and one make three." If such knowledge is fluent, children may be able to use it to solve a more complex unknown addend problem, for example, "Two and how many make three?" ("One.")

For numbers larger than they can visualize, children will need to use objects or fingers to carry out a counting-all or taking-away solution procedure. Children will learn new additions and subtractions as they have such experiences. The doubles that involve the same addends (2 is 1 and 1, 4 is 2 and 2, 6 is 3 and 3, 8 is 4 and 4) are particularly easy for children to learn. The visual 5-groups (e.g., 8 is made from 5 and 3) discussed for the number core are also helpful in adding and subtracting.

Research indicates that at present, many 4s/pre-Ks from lower-income backgrounds cannot solve problems given just in number words ("What is two and one?" or "What is three take away one?") even with very small numbers. Such children need opportunities to learn and practice adding and subtracting methods for such problems with objects and with fingers. Experience composing/decomposing numbers to be able to see the partners hiding inside the small numbers 3, 4, 5 is also helpful. Such alternating focusing on the total and then on the partners (addends) will enable children to answer problems given only in number words and relate addition and subtraction as opposite operations.

Making Up Addition and Subtraction Stories

1) Children can pretend that blocks are different things and make up story problems.

Sam: *"Here is one girl playing at the park."*

Sam: *"Now two more girls come to play. Now there are three girls at the park."*

The teacher can help children ask a question, because that is the hardest part.

Teacher: *"You just told us how many in all. Can you ask a question about your story so that Maria can answer it? How many ..."* (pause to allow child to continue)

Sam: *"How many girls ... "* (pause, uncertain)

Teacher: *"Can someone help?"*

Lucy: *"How many girls in all?"*

Teacher: *"Thanks, Lucy. Sam, can you say your question now?"*

Sam: *"How many girls are at the park?"*

2) Children can also draw circles to show an addition situation.

Taryn: *"Here are three cats and two cats. There are five cats in all."*

Drawing the solution actions using circles or other simple shapes instead of pictures of real objects can be helpful for later 4s/pre-Ks. The two addends can be separated just by space, or encircled separately, or separated by a vertical line segment. Some children can also begin to make mathematics drawings to show their solutions. Teacher and child drawings leave a visual record of the full solution that facilitates children's reflecting on the solution and discussing and explaining it. For children, making mathematics drawings is also a creative activity in which the child is somehow showing in space actions that occur over time. Children make these drawings in various interesting ways that can lead to productive discussions. These young children also enjoy drawing more realistic pictures of problem situations. This approach is a good way for them to present problem situations to other children who can then describe the situation in words. Such pictures can help build meanings for everyone. But drawing time-consuming pictures should not be encouraged for problem solving; simplified mathematics drawings are faster and focus more on the mathematically important aspects of the situation.

Activities on Breaking Numbers Apart into Partners

1) Show a child 6 counters and a large card with a line drawn down the middle (or use a stick as a separator).

Adult: "I can make 6 with 3 and 3."

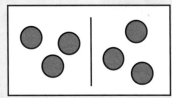

Remove the counters.

Adult: "Show me other ways to make 6 with partners."
Katie: "I can make 6 with 5 and 1."

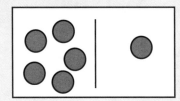

2) Show 6 dinosaurs and count them together.

Hide some by covering with a box or plate. Then ask how many are hiding.

Number Lines Are Not Appropriate for 2s/3s, 4s/Pre-Ks, or Grade 1 Children

A great deal of confusion arises about what the term *number line* means. Two NRC reports (Kilpatrick, Swafford, and Findell 2001; Cross, Woods, and Schweingruber 2009) recommend that number lines not be used until grade 2 because they are conceptually too difficult for younger children. In early childhood materials, the term *number line* or *mental number line* often really means a *number path*, such as in the common early childhood games where numbers are put on squares and children move along such a numbered path. Such number paths are count models in which things are counted. Each square is a thing that can be counted, so these are appropriate for children from age 2 through grade 1. A number path and a number line are shown in figure 2.6 along with the meanings that children must understand and relate when using these models. In contrast, a *number line* is a length model, such as a ruler or a bar graph, in which numbers are represented by the length from zero along a line segmented into equal lengths. Children need to count the length units, not the numbers. Young children have difficulties with such a number-line representation because they have difficulty seeing the units—they need to see things, so they focus on the numbers or the segmenting marks instead of on the lengths. Thus they may count the starting point 0 and then be off by one. Or they may focus on the spaces and be confused by the location of the numbers at the end of the spaces.

It is important to show in classrooms for young children a *number list* (a list of numbers in order) or a *number path* (a list of numbers inside identical objects, such as the squares in figure 2.6). Or the numbers can be beside the objects. Groupings that show these numbers can also be shown (e.g., the 5-groups can be above the numbers 6 through 10). Children can play games and count along such number paths or number lists. But number lines should be avoided because they are confusing. Learning to count to ten and understand the written number symbols are facilitated by games such as the number-path game in Ramani and Siegler (2008). In this game, children say the numbers on which they are landing (e.g., "I got 2, so I count the next two squares: Six, seven") instead of the usual counting of the number they rolled or spun (e.g., "I got 2, so I count two squares: One, two").

Table 2.2 of addition/subtraction solution methods shows how children will come to use the number-word list (the number-word sequence) as a *mental tool* for solving addition and subtraction problems. They are able in grades 1 and 2 to use increasingly abbreviated and abstract solution methods, such as the counting-on and the make-a-ten methods. At this point the number words themselves have become unitized mental objects to be added, subtracted, and ordered. The original separate sequence, counting, and cardinal meanings have become related and finally integrated over several years into a *truly numerical mental number-word sequence.* Each number can be seen as embedded within each successive number and as seriated: related to the numbers before and after it by a linear ordering created by the order relation

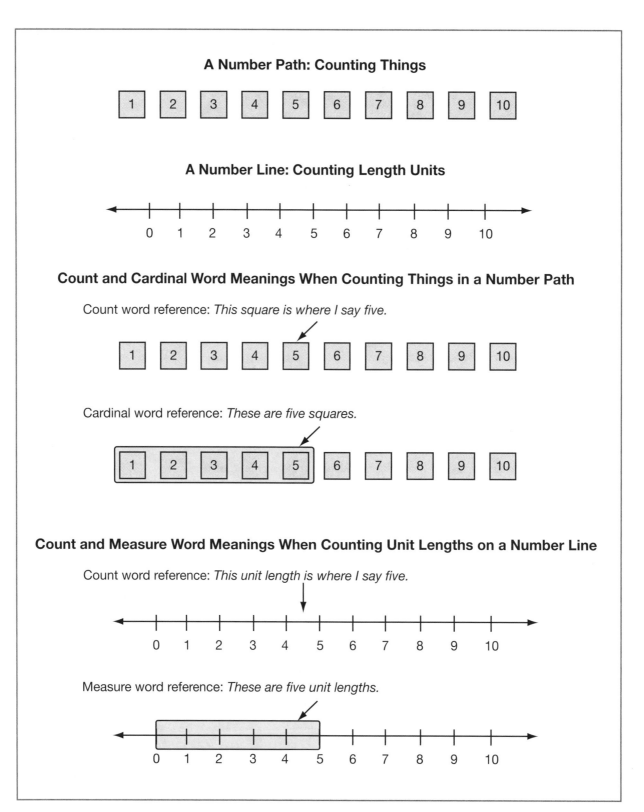

A Number Path: Counting Things

A Number Line: Counting Length Units

Count and Cardinal Word Meanings When Counting Things in a Number Path

Count word reference: *This square is where I say five.*

Cardinal word reference: *These are five squares.*

Count and Measure Word Meanings When Counting Unit Lengths on a Number Line

Count word reference: *This unit length is where I say five.*

Measure word reference: *These are five unit lengths.*

Fig. 2.6. A number path and a number line

less than applied to each pair of numbers. This is what Piaget (1941/1965) called *truly operational cardinal number:* any number within the sequence displays both class inclusion (the embeddedness) and seriation (see also Kamii [1985]). But this fully Piagetian integrated sequence will not be finished for most children until grade 1 or grade 2, when they can do at least some of the step 3 derived-fact solution methods. These methods depend on the whole teaching-learning path discussed in the foregoing and presented in more detail in *Focus in Grade 1* (NCTM, forthcoming) and *Focus in Grade 2* (NCTM, forthcoming).

Many researchers have noted how the number-word list turns into a mental representational tool for adding and subtracting. A few researchers have called this a *mental number line.* However, for young children this is a misnomer because children in kindergarten and grade 1 are using a *mental number-word list* (sequence) as a count model: each number word is taken as a unit to be counted, matched, added, or subtracted.

The use of number lines, such as in a ruler or a bar-graph scale, is an important part of measurement and is discussed in that section. In grade 2, these tools all form an appropriate important part of the learning goals. But they are too complex for many children at earlier ages.

3 Geometry, Spatial Reasoning, and Measurement

Geometry, spatial reasoning, and measurement are essential areas in children's development. From birth, children use shape to understand the world. Shape is a core component in geometry, with spatial reasoning a complementary component. Spatial reasoning includes spatial orientation—knowing how to get around in the world—and spatial visualization—knowing how to build and manipulate objects mentally, including composing and decomposing objects. Geometric measurement rounds out the core components. *Geometry* means "earth measure," and geometry, spatial reasoning, and measurement are topics that connect with each other and with other mathematics as well as connect mathematics with real-world situations. For example, these core components are the foundations of number lines, arrays in multiplication, fractions, graphing, and topics beyond. They also lie at the heart of physics, chemistry, biology, geology and geography, art, and architecture.

Unfortunately, geometry and measurement are two of U.S. students' weakest topics in mathematics. Even in the preschool years, children in the U.S. know less about shape than children in other countries. Fortunately, they know enough to build on, they can learn a lot quickly, and they enjoy engaging with shapes, space, and measurements. Indeed, young children play with shape naturally. In a study of the mathematics children engage in spontaneously in their play, the most frequent dealt with shapes and patterns. Teachers can help young children develop their spatial reasoning and their understanding of shapes and measurement by talking with them about these elements in their play and by building on their engagement with nature through planned activities and discussions that stimulate children's thinking.

Shape and Structure: Overview

From the earliest years, children learn about shape and use shapes to learn. In learning the *geometry* of shapes, they progress through different levels of thinking about shapes. For example, at first, they cannot explicitly distinguish circles, triangles, and squares from nonexamples. They gradually develop richer visual templates for these categories and eventually learn about the parts and attributes of the shapes. Teachers can foster children's development by providing rich examples and experiences.

Table 3.1 presents the developmental progressions for the ideas and skills of geometry and spatial reasoning.

Shape and structure: 2s/3s

Children initially form visual templates, or models, of shapes. These templates vary depending on the quality of their experiences. Without *good* experiences, children learn inaccurate, rigid, and limited notions. For example,

Table 3.1

Progression of Ideas and Skills for Geometry, Spatial Reasoning, and Measurement

Prekindergarten	Kindergarten	Grade 1
Shape and Structure	**Shape and Structure**	**Shape and Structure**
2s/3s: Recognize two-dimensional shapes informally (including at least circles, squares, then triangles, rectangles) in different orientations. Discriminate between two-dimensional and three-dimensional shapes intuitively, marked by accurate matching or naming. See and describe pictures of objects (e.g., recognize a three-dimensional object on a two-dimensional page of a book). 4s/pre-Ks: Recognize and describe two-dimensional shapes regardless of orientation, size, and shape (including circles and half-/quarter-circles, squares and rectangles, triangles, and regular rhombuses, trapezoids, hexagons). Describe shapes by number of sides and/or corners (up to the number they can count) and sides of same or different length. Describe the difference between two-dimensional and three-dimensional shapes, and name common three-dimensional shapes informally or with mathematical names ("ball"/sphere; "box" or rectangular prism; "rectangular block" or "triangular block"; "can"/cylinder).	Recognize and describe a wide variety of two-dimensional shapes (e.g., octagons, parallelograms, convex/concave figures) regardless of orientation, size, and shape. Sort shapes by number of sides and/or corners and length relationships between sides. Recognize and name common three-dimensional shapes (including real-world objects), including spheres, cylinders, [rectangular] prisms, and pyramids.	Name most common shapes, including rhombuses, without making mistakes, such as calling ovals circles. Recognize (at least) right angles, so distinguishing between a rectangle and a parallelogram without right angles. Use manipulatives representing parts of shapes, such as sides and angle "connectors," to make a shape that is completely correct on the basis of knowledge of components and relationships.
Spatial Relations	**Spatial Relations**	**Spatial Relations**
2s/3s: Enact spatial movements informally, using such relational terms as *up, down, on, off,* and *under.* 4s/pre-Ks: Match shapes by intuitively using geometric motions to superimpose them. Use relational words of proximity, such as *beside, next to,* and *between,* referring to a two-dimensional environment. Match the faces of three-dimensional shapes to two-dimensional shapes, naming the two-dimensional shapes.	Begin to use relational language of *right* and *left.* Identify and create symmetric figures (e.g., mirrors as reflections).	Use geometric motions to create symmetric figures (e.g., paper folding; also mirrors as reflections) and determine congruence.
Compositions and Decompositions in Space	**Compositions and Decompositions in Space**	**Compositions and Decompositions in Space**
2s/3s: Solve simple puzzles involving things in the world. Create pictures by representing single objects, each with a different shape. Combine unit blocks by stacking.	Create pattern-block designs (those with multiples of 60 degree and 120 degree angles). Create compositions and complete puzzles with systematicity and anticipation, using a variety of shape sets (e.g., pattern blocks; rectangular grids with squares, right triangles, and rectangles; tangrams). Build simple three-dimensional structures from pictured models.	Make new two-dimensional shapes and shape structures out of smaller shapes and substitute groups of shapes for other shapes to create new shapes in different ways. (See related area goals.)

Prekindergarten	Kindergarten	Grade 1
Compositions and Decompositions in Space	**Compositions and Decompositions in Space**	**Compositions and Decompositions in Space**
4s/pre-Ks: Move shapes using slides and flips, and turn them to combine shapes to build pictures. Copy a design shown on a grid, placing squares and rectangles onto squared grid paper. Combine building blocks, using multiple spatial relations to produce composite shapes (arches, enclosures, corners, and crosses).		
Concept of Measurement	**Concept of Measurement**	**Concept of Measurement**
2s/3s: Identify two-dimensional and three-dimensional objects as "the same" or "different" in size. 4s/pre-Ks: Identify objects and drawings as "more" or "less" on the basis of attributes they can identify (and later can measure), such as length and area, and solve problems by making direct comparisons of objects on the basis of those attributes.	Use measurable attributes, such as length or area, to solve problems by comparing and ordering objects.	Compose and decompose plane and solid shapes, thus building an understanding of part-whole relationships and developing the background for working with units composed of units. (These concepts relate to the geometry goals.)
Length	**Length**	**Length**
2s/3s: Intuitively recognize length as extent of one-dimensional space. Compare two objects directly, noting equality or inequality. 4s/pre-Ks: Begin to measure by laying units end to end. Understand that lengths can be concatenated to make a new length.	Compare the lengths of two objects both directly (by comparing them with each other) and indirectly (by comparing both with a third object), and order several objects according to length (even if differences between consecutive lengths are small). Measure by laying units end to end, covering the whole without gaps, and count the units to find the total length.	Measure by repeated use of a unit, and apply the resulting measures to comparison situations.
Area	**Area**	**Area**
2s/3s: Use side-matching strategies in comparing areas. 4s/pre-Ks: Compare areas for tasks that suggest superposition or show decomposition into squares.	Cover a rectangular region with square units. Count squares in rectangular arrays correctly and (increasingly) systematically.	Make and draw coverings of simple rectangular regions with square units. For rectangles two squares high or wide, count the rows or columns of two by twos.
Volume	**Volume**	**Volume**
2s/3s: Identify capacity or volume as an attribute. 4s/pre-Ks: Compare two containers directly by pouring.	Compare two containers using a third container and (at least implicitly) transitive reasoning. Fill rectangular containers with cubes and/or make rectangular prisms ("buildings") from layers of blocks.	Fill rectangular containers with cubes, completing one layer at a time, and/or make rectangular prisms ("buildings") from layers of blocks.

Note: Some composition and decomposition activities overlap with measurement (area and volume).

Note: Grade 3 develops the foregoing area work as a setting for multiplication. A more complete development of area is a grade 4 Focal Point, and a more complete development of volume is a grade 5 Focal Point.

many children only see equilateral (all sides and angles equal in measure) or isosceles triangles (at least two sides equal), always with a horizontal base. Their templates and their informal notions of triangles become rigid, limited to that presentation of "triangle."

Children build more accurate models of shapes if they experience wider varieties of each shape category. Playing with triangles that are, as children say, "long and skinny" as well as those that are equilateral will promote rich mental models.

If shapes are presented to children in categories, what order might be most helpful? Research suggests some guidelines. All people tend to prefer symmetric shapes. The circle and square are therefore easy to recognize and name early. Then triangles might be introduced. No problem arises with *first* introducing children to typical instances (equilateral triangles, even with one side horizontal), because that may help them form the initial model. As soon as possible, however, they should begin to see, feel, and play with a variety of shapes in a variety of sizes and positions within each category. Children two to three years of age are not too young for this of type of learning. In one study, one of the youngest three-year-olds scored higher than every six-year-old identifying a wide variety of shapes. Such children have good experiences with shapes, including rich, varied examples and nonexamples. Teachers can extend and develop children's thinking by providing such varied shapes for children to explore and by discussing the qualities and attributes of those shapes.

Presentations of shapes to very young children should include wondering about where various shapes can be found in the world, including finding two-dimensional shapes (e.g., rectangles) on three-dimensional shapes (boxes, blocks, tables, etc.). Children also learn to recognize familiar three-dimensional shapes in two-dimensional pictures of them, as in picture books (e.g., "that's a ball [sphere]"). Although they may name a three-dimensional shape by the name of one of its faces (e.g., calling a cube a "square"), their ability to match two dimensions to corresponding two dimensions (and similarly for three dimensions) indicates their intuitive differentiation of two-dimensional and three-dimensional shapes. Naming these shapes differently and finding the "hidden" two-dimensional shape in the three-dimensional solids can help them learn to understand this essential difference explicitly.

Shape and structure: 4s/pre-Ks

Preschool children form visual templates, or models, of shape categories. For example, children recognize a shape as a rectangle because "it looks like a door." As with 2s/3s, because children base their understanding of shapes on examples, they need to experience a rich variety of shapes in each shape category so that their mental models are not overly restricted. Children should see examples of rectangles that are long and skinny as well as in different positions and orientations, and examples of triangles that have sides of three different lengths (see fig. 3.1 and fig. 3.2).

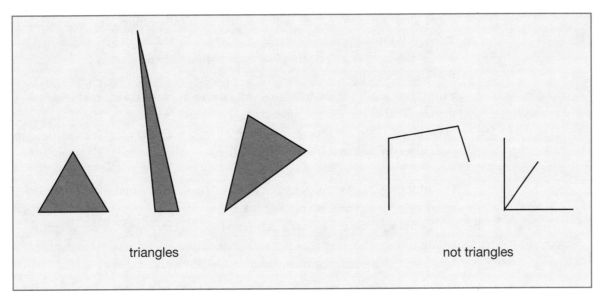

Fig. 3.1. Triangles and nontriangles

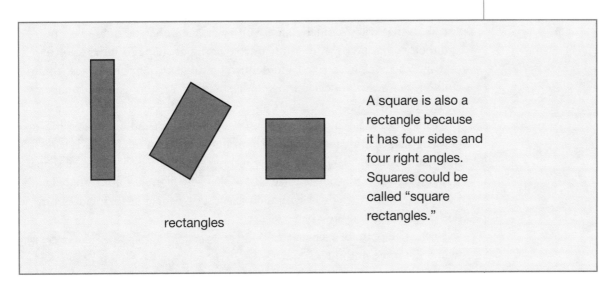

A square is also a rectangle because it has four sides and four right angles. Squares could be called "square rectangles."

Fig. 3.2. Rectangles

Children also need to see examples of shapes beyond circles, squares, rectangles, and triangles. Without these, children develop limited notions. For example, many children come to believe incorrectly that a geometric figure such as a trapezoid "is not a shape" because it is not a shape for which they know a name (and many know only circle, square, triangle, and rectangle).

So, just as with younger children, preschoolers need high-quality experiences with shapes. They should recognize a wide variety of shapes, including shapes that are different sizes and are presented in different orientations (e.g., squares and triangles rotated so that their bases are not horizontal). This is a crucial extension of the early visual level of thinking that should continue throughout education, even as more mathematically explicit and sophisticated levels of thinking take precedence.

In the same vein, preschoolers learn to describe the differences between two-dimensional and three-dimensional shapes informally. They also learn to name common three-dimensional shapes informally and with mathematical names ("ball"/sphere; "box" or rectangular prism; "rectangular block" or "triangular block"; "can"/cylinder). They initially use their own terms and language and increasingly adopt mathematical language. For example, "diamond" gives way to "rhombus" and "corners" becomes "vertices" (or "angles" if the sides or size of the angles is considered). Faces of three-dimensional shapes are identified as specific two-dimensional shapes.

Forming accurate and flexible mental models for shapes is important for children at any age. But it is not sufficient. Children, especially when just forming such visual templates, often do not think about shapes in terms of their parts or attributes (properties). Preschoolers can begin this kind of thinking, for example, building shapes from physical models of line segments. At this level, it is a challenge for children to integrate those parts into a coherent whole, but their constructive activity will help them learn the concepts and skills that will eventually merge into a robust understanding of shapes and their components. A mature understanding of shape includes knowing that shapes are characterized and defined by some of their properties. Young children can begin to develop this understanding for some kinds of shapes, for example, when they identify a shape as a triangle *because* it has three sides.

Instructional activities that promote such reflection and discussion include building shapes from components. For example, children might build shapes from parts, such as making squares or rectangles and three-dimensional shapes-from different lengths of sticks (see fig. 3.3). They might also form shapes with their bodies, either singly or with their friends. Of course, shapes made from one's body are not always the most accurate. The point of such activities lies more in thinking and talking about what must be done to build the shapes. Returning to building shapes with sticks, children might discuss how to construct geometric figures even more accurately, with more understanding of the relationships among the parts.

Another sequence of activities involves tactile-kinesthetic exploration of shapes (feeling shapes hidden in a box). Such nonvisual exploration of shapes does not allow simple visual matching-to-typical examples.

Fig. 3.3. Building three-dimensional shapes with toothpicks

Instead, they require children to carefully put the parts of the shape into relationship with each other. First, adults or peers might place a small number of shapes on the table and secretly hide a shape congruent to one of these in a box. Children feel the shape and point to the matching shape, then pull out the hidden shape to check. Later, children do not have the shapes on the table. Instead, they have to name the shape they are feeling.

Such activities help children learn to identify and describe shapes by the number of their sides or corners. This is illustrated by a preschooler who declared that an obtuse triangle "must be a triangle, because it has three sides." Such descriptions build geometric concepts but also reasoning skills and language. They encourage children to view shapes analytically. Children begin to describe some shapes in terms of their properties, such as saying that squares have four sides of *equal length*. They informally describe properties of blocks in functional contexts, such as that some blocks roll and others do not. "Math Talk about Shapes" (below) illustrates teachers' questions that help children develop these linguistic and mathematical competences.

Math Talk about Shapes

Drawings

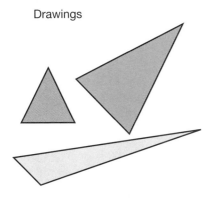

Plastic or wooden shapes that can be moved

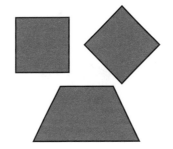

Teacher: "What shape is this?"

Child: "A triangle!"

Teacher: "How can you tell?"

Child: "It has three sides and three points."

Possible teacher questions and comments:

"Which of these shapes are squares?"

"How can you tell that this shape [point to second shape] is a square?"

"Is this shape [point to second shape] like this one [point to the first shape]? How can you tell?"

"Do these two shapes [point to first two shapes] match? See if they match!"

"The corners of squares are special because exactly four fit together."

The recommended approaches and activities in this section have been carried out successfully with three- and four-year-olds in care centers or classrooms serving low- and middle-income children, with strong positive results on children's learning.

Spatial Relations: Overview

Reasoning about spatial relations includes two main spatial abilities: spatial orientation and spatial visualization and imagery. Other important competencies include knowing how to represent spatial ideas and how and when to apply such abilities in solving problems.

Spatial orientation involves knowing where you are and how to get around in the world. Similar to number, spatial orientation is a core cognitive domain—humans have competencies from birth. Children's skills are initially based on their own position and their movements through space, and soon increasingly include external references. Adults and educators need to help them *mathematize* these early competencies.

Spatial visualization involves building and manipulating objects mentally. Images are internal representations of objects that are structurally similar to their real-world counterparts. An image is not a "picture in the head." It is more abstract, more malleable, and less crisp than a picture. It is often segmented into parts. The spatial visualization considered here involves understanding and performing imagined movements of two- and three-dimensional geometric objects. Children need to be able to create a mental image and manipulate it.

Spatial relations: 2s/3s

Language for spatial relationships is acquired in a consistent sequence. The first terms acquired are *in, on,* and *under,* along with such vertical directionality terms as *up* and *down.* These terms initially refer to transformations. That is, *on* is not initially used to describe a smaller object on top of another, but only as making one object become physically attached to another object. Second, children learn words describing closeness, such as *beside.* Third, children learn words referring to objects in relation to a frame of reference that includes objects and the self, such as *in front of* and *behind.* The words *left* and *right* are learned much later and are the source of confusion for several years, up to age seven or eight years.

From the first year of life, children develop increasing implicit ability to move objects. The more they are encouraged to move themselves through large spaces, move objects around, and *talk* about these movements, the more children will develop both spatial orientation and spatial visualization abilities. They also can learn to apply that vocabulary both in three-dimensional contexts and in two-dimensional situations, such as the "bottom" of a picture that they are drawing on a horizontal surface. Teachers can encourage children's spatial reasoning and vocabulary development in several ways. They can describe what children are doing, ask them about their work ("Is the doorway in your block building tall enough for the truck to get through?"), and ask them for spatial descriptions ("*Where* did you put the truck she wanted?").

Spatial relations: 4s/pre-Ks

In these early years, adults can help children learn to analyze what others need to hear to follow a path or route through space. Such learning is dependent on relevant experiences, including language. For more complex routes, language is often not as helpful as physical models or drawings.

To build spatial orientation skills, educational environments can include interesting layouts at home, in the neighborhood, and inside classrooms. Incidental and planned experiences with landmarks and routes, and frequent verbalizations about spatial relations and spatial movements (*forward, back*), finding a missing object ("under the table that's next to the door"), putting objects away, and finding the way back home from an excursion. Verbal interaction is particularly important, as in "it's in the large bag under the table." "Activtity on Spatial Relationships" (below) provides other suggestions.

Activity on Spatial Relationships

Teacher:

"Find the matching circle that is **on** the table, next to the tissue box."

"Find the matching square that is **under** the chair."

"Find the matching triangle that is **inside** the box under the table."

Preschoolers can build simple, but meaningful, models of spatial relationships with such toys as houses, cars, and trees, as well as with blocks. Children might use cutout shapes of a tree, swing set, and sandbox in the playground and lay them out on a felt board as a simple map.

In these activities, preschoolers extend their vocabulary of spatial relations with such terms as *beside, next to* and *between*, which can apply to both three-dimensional and two-dimensional spaces. Later, they extend this vocabulary to terms that involve frames of reference, such as *to the side of* or *in front of*.

Preschoolers can learn to check whether pairs of two-dimensional shapes are congruent by using geometry motions intuitively, moving from less accurate strategies such as side-matching or the use of lengths to the use of superimposition—placing one shape on top of the other. Children extend this initially intuitive knowledge to use the geometric motions of slides, flips, and turns explicitly and intentionally in discussing their solutions to puzzles or in applying such motions in computer environments to manipulate shapes. They can learn to predict the effects of geometric motions—often initially using computer environments.

Children also begin to be able to cover a rectangular space with physical tiles and represent their tilings with simple drawings, although they may initially leave gaps in each and may not align all the squares. This competence is mainly one of spatial structuring, but it has close connections with the ability to construct compositions in two-dimensional space.

Preschoolers also learn about the parts of three-dimensional shapes by using motions to match the faces of three-dimensional shapes to two-dimensional shapes and representing two-dimensional and three-dimensional relationships with objects. For example, they may make a simple model of the classroom using a rectangular block for the teacher's desk, small cubes for chairs, and so forth.

This and many other activities develop spatial visualization abilities. Manipulative work with shapes, such as tangrams, pattern blocks, and other shape sets, lays a valuable foundation. Computers are especially helpful, as the screen tools make motions more accessible to reflection and thus bring them to an explicit level of awareness for children.

Many shape activities also develop spatial visualization. One especially useful series of activities are the tactile-kinesthetic exploration of shapes. Also important are building and composing with two- and three-dimensional shapes, aspects of the core component to which we now turn.

Compositions and Decompositions in Space: Overview

The abilities involved in putting together and taking apart shapes are important for many reasons. These geometric competencies are at the foundation of geometry but also of arithmetic. Children who can compose shapes develop better understanding of composing and decomposing numbers, such as 7 as 6 + 1 or 5 + 2, and they will be better able to understand arrays in multiplication as being composing of rows and columns (e.g., five rows with seven squares in each row). Composing and decomposing shapes are also important in measurement and higher-order geometric work, as well as in such fields as architecture and the visual arts. Putting shapes together to make a new unit that can be repeated in a pattern is useful in geometry and measurement and is part of a general mathematical process of joining units to make new units.

Compositions and decompositions in space: 2s/3s

Young children can solve simple puzzles involving things in the world, such as wooden puzzles with insets for each animal or building. They create pictures with geometric shapes (circles, circle sections, and polygons), often representing single objects with different shapes but eventually combining shapes to make, for example, the body of a vehicle or animal. That is, initially children manipulate individual shapes but are unable to combine them to compose a larger shape. For example, children might use a single shape for a sun, a separate shape for a tree, and another separate shape for a person.

Later, children learn to place two-dimensional shapes contiguously to form pictures. In free-form "make a picture" tasks, for example, each shape used represents a unique role, or function, in the picture. For example, each shape may represent one "body part" of a person: a head, arm, or leg. Children can fill simple frame-based "shapes puzzles" using trial and error.

Composition with three-dimensional shapes usually begins with stacking blocks. Children can then learn to stack *congruent* blocks and make horizontal "lines," such as a road. Next they build a vertical and horizontal structure, such as a "floor" or simple "wall." Later, some three-year-olds begin to extend their buildings in multiple directions, possibly creating arches, enclosures, corners, and crosses, but often using unsystematic trial and error and simple addition of pieces.

Compositions and decompositions in space: 4s/pre-Ks

Preschoolers can place shapes contiguously to form pictures in which several shapes play a single role. For example, a long body or a leg might be created from three squares laid side-by-side. Children choose shapes using overall shape or the length of one side. They can rotate and flip shapes by using trial-and-error to attempt different arrangements. Thus, they initially use a "pick, try it out, and discard" strategy.

With experience, many preschoolers begin to anticipate which shapes will fit on the basis of shape and angle size as well as side lengths. The equilateral triangle "world" of pattern blocks provides a "microworld" in which matching by sides (all of which are equal in length or double the unit length), fitting angles (multiples of 30 degrees), and composing (two equilateral triangles can "make" the blue rhombus, a rhombus and a triangle make a trapezoid, etc.) are helpful at this level. (See "Some Relationships among Pattern Tiles" on the next page for an illustration of relationships within this microworld.) Rotation and flipping are used more intentionally to select and place shapes.

Related to their ability to tile the rectangular section of a plane, children copy and make designs from squares, placing these shapes onto squared grid

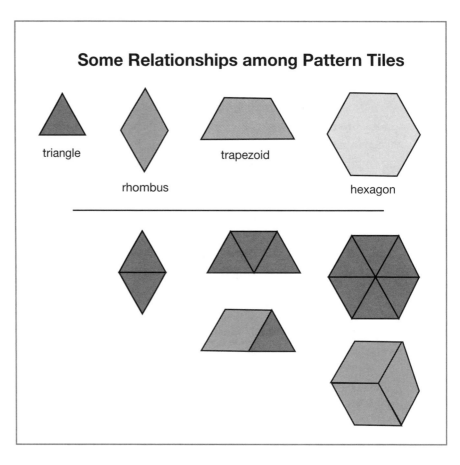

paper (see fig. 3.4). This square-based microworld is similarly simple and thus facilitates composition, but it also develops the foundations of much of mathematics (spatial structuring, multiplication, area, volume, coordinates, etc.).

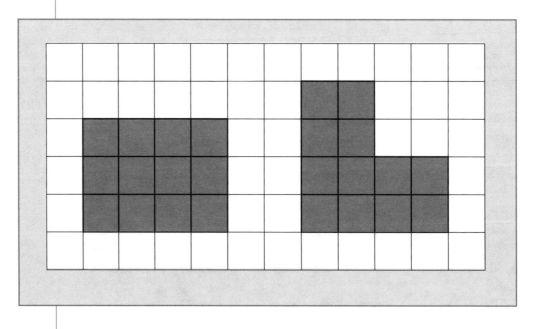

Fig. 3.4. Making designs from squares

By using three-dimensional shapes, preschoolers combine building blocks using multiple spatial relations, extending in multiple directions and with multiple points of contact among components, showing flexibility in integrating parts of the structure. Thus, they can reliably produce arches, enclosures, corners, and crosses, including enclosures that are several blocks in height. Later, they can learn to compose building blocks with anticipation, understanding what three-dimensional shape will be produced with a composition of two or more other (simple, familiar) three-dimensional shapes.

Manipulatives are essential in this work. Interestingly, computer software can provide a parallel set of experiences that are just as real and helpful to young children as physical manipulatives. In fact, high-quality software programs may have specific advantages. For example, some computer manipulatives offer more flexibility than their noncomputer counterparts. Computer-based pattern blocks, for example, can be composed and decomposed in more ways than physical pattern blocks. For example, the green triangle might break in half. As another example, children and teachers can save and later retrieve any arrangement of computer manipulatives. As a final illustration, computers can help children become aware of and mathematize their actions. For example, very young children can move puzzle pieces into place, but they do not think about their actions. In making decisions in computer settings, children become aware of and describe these motions, especially when their teacher asks them to describe what they did—perhaps to help a classmate.

Measurement

Geometric measurement[1] connects and enriches the two most important topics for early mathematics, geometry and number. Children's understanding of measurement has its roots in infancy and the preschool years but grows over many years. Measurement often develops from a need to compare two or more objects, for example, which box is bigger?

Table 3.1 presents the developmental progressions for the ideas and skills of measurement.

Length: overview

Length is a characteristic of an object found by quantifying how far it is between two endpoints. *Distance* is often used similarly to quantify how far it is between two points in space. Measuring length or distance consists of two aspects: identifying a unit of measure and *subdividing* the object by that unit, placing that unit end to end ("iterating") alongside the object.

---

1. In this section, we describe children's development of *geometric* measurement—measurement in one, two, and three dimensions. We do not consider measurement of nongeometric attributes, such as weight/mass, capacity, time, and color, because these are more appropriately considered in science and social studies curricula.

Length: 2s/3s

Even the youngest children naturally encounter and discuss quantities. They learn to use words that represent quantity or magnitude of a certain attribute. They compare two objects directly and recognize—intuitively—their equality or inequality (e.g., "It's not fair. You have more!").

Young children naturally describe and compare continuous quantities, such as length, in their play. They first learn to use words that represent quantity or magnitude of a certain attribute. Facilitating this language is important not only to develop communication abilities but for the development of mathematical concepts. Simply using labels such as "big/little/tiny" helped children as young as three years represent and apply ordering, or seriating, abilities, even in the face of distracting visual factors.

Children begin by informally recognizing length as the extent of one-dimensional space. For example, they might remark of a road made with building blocks, "This is *long*." They also might compose lengths intuitively, as when they join two block roads to make "a *really long* road." They can then compare two objects directly and recognize and describe their equality. For example, they might say, "You are just as tall as I am!" They are perhaps even more sensitive to *in*equality, as in, "My pencil is longer than yours."

Length: 4s/pre-Ks

Preschoolers can be guided to learn important measurement concepts if provided appropriate experiences. Most can learn to overcome perceptual cues and make progress in reasoning about and measuring quantities. They are ready to learn important measurement concepts, connecting number with the quantity. Note that this readiness stands in stark contrast with the average U.S. child, who has experienced limited measurement tasks and who exhibits limited understanding of measurement until after the primary grades.

Preschoolers can begin to learn two different length-related skills. The first involves comparing the length of two objects. First, children might compare them directly. They can also begin to compare them using a third object and transitive reasoning. This "indirect comparison" might be verbalized with such language as "the desk is shorter than my full arm, and the doorway is wider, so I'm sure the desk will fit."

Using language to highlight the differences between counting-based terms (e.g., "two trucks") and terms referring to measurable attributes (e.g., "a longer piece of string") can help children form relationships between counting and continuous measurement.

The second important length-related skill that preschoolers can begin to learn involves actual measurement. For example, they might lay physical units, such as centimeter manipulatives, end to end and count them to measure a length. At first, some children may not recognize the need for equal-length units and initially may make such errors as leaving gaps between units. Teachers can help children develop those concepts by applying the resulting measures to comparison situations.

Area: overview

The area of a shape is a measure of the amount of space inside the shape; it tells us how much material is needed to cover the shape (see fig. 3.5). Area measurement assumes that a suitable two-dimensional region is chosen as a unit, congruent regions have equal areas, regions do not overlap, and the area of the union of two regions that do not overlap is the sum of their areas. Finding the area of a region can be thought of as tiling a region with a two-dimensional unit of measure. To understand area effectively, children need to develop spatial structuring—the mental operation of organizing space into rows and columns. Such understandings are complex, and children develop them over time. These area understandings do not develop well in traditional U.S. instruction and have not done so for a long time.

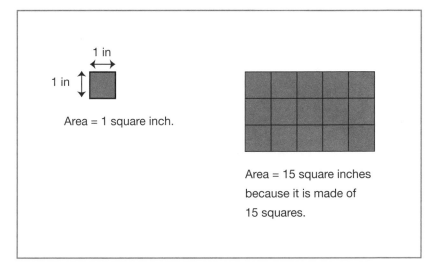

Fig. 3.5. Area

Area: 2s/3s

Perhaps the most important experiences for the youngest child are to play with structured materials, from square tiles to blocks to puzzles (see the section on composing and decomposing geometric shapes).

Teachers might also discuss area in everyday settings. Making use of a common experience when children first paint at an easel, one teacher remarked, "You covered the *whole* piece of paper with blue!"

Area: 4s/pre-Ks

Preschoolers also begin to be able to cover a rectangular space with physical tiles intentionally. Some begin to represent their tilings with simple drawings, although they may leave gaps in each and may not align all the squares. "Rectangle Puzzles" on the next page suggests puzzles that children will find interesting.

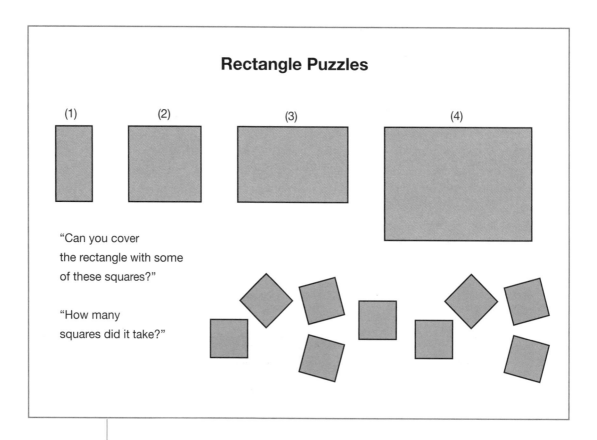

Volume: overview

The volume of a three-dimensional shape is a measure of the amount of material or space enclosed within the shape (see fig. 3.6). Volume introduces even more complexity than area. Adding a third dimension presents a significant challenge to students' spatial structuring—students need to think of rows, columns, and *layers* (height).

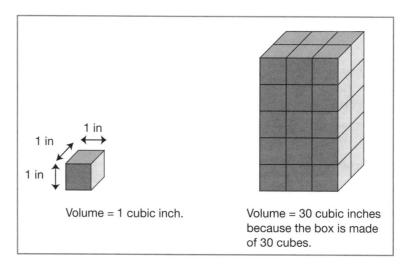

Fig. 3.6. Volume

Volume can also involve liquids or solids. This fact leads to two ways to measure volume, illustrated by "packing" a space such as a three-dimensional array with cubic units and "filling" with iterations of a fluid unit that takes the shape of the container. For filling, the unit structure may be perceived as one-dimensional by some children. For example, children may simply count the scoops of sand that fill a jar. They may not process this quantity as three-dimensional.

Volume: 2s/3s

Again, the most important experiences for the youngest child are to play with structured materials, including building blocks and cubes (see the section on composing and decomposing geometric shapes).

Volume: 4s/pre-Ks

Children can compare the volume of containers informally by pouring (water, sand, etc.) from one to the other (filling volume). They can fill boxes with cubes or make buildings that have layers of rectangular arrays (packing volume; see the illustration in "Filling Open-Top Boxes with Cubes" below).

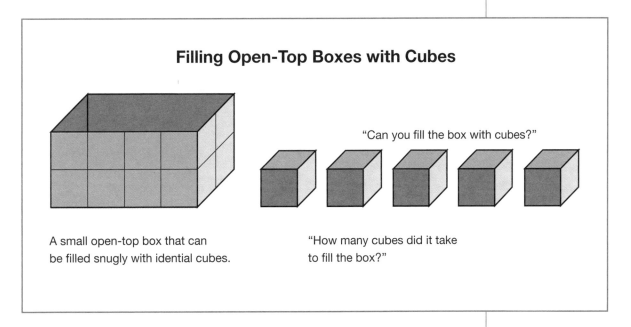

Filling Open-Top Boxes with Cubes

A small open-top box that can be filled snugly with identical cubes.

"Can you fill the box with cubes?"

"How many cubes did it take to fill the box?"

Geometry, Spatial Reasoning, and Measurement: Final Words

Geometric and spatial experiences are appropriate for, and achievable by, young children. They also contribute to their overall mathematical development. Each of several recently developed, research-based preschool mathematics curricula includes substantive geometric and spatial activities, with some of these featuring such a focus in 40 percent or more of the activities. Field testing has shown that these activities were achievable by, and motivating to, young children. Formal evaluations reveal that such activities contribute to children's development of both numerical and spatial/geometric concepts. Curricula that include substantial spatial and geometric activities show remarkably positive results. Children gain in geometric and spatial skills and show pronounced benefits in the areas of arithmetic and writing readiness in primary school. Children are better prepared for all school tasks when they gain the thinking tools and representational competence of geometric and spatial sense.

4 Mathematizing:
Solving Problems, Reasoning, and Communicating, Connecting, and Representing Ideas in Prekindergarten

The general processes of problem solving, reasoning, and communicating, connecting, and representing ideas are important at every grade level and in all topics in mathematics. To make sense of mathematics and to connect mathematics to the world around them, students at all levels must actively think about mathematical ideas and seek to connect the ideas to their existing knowledge. To extend their knowledge, students at all levels must solve new problems, and they must discuss their solution strategies and ideas with others so that they can examine and refine those strategies and ideas. Teachers are important in these processes because they can set expectations about mathematics: that mathematics is a sense-making enterprise, that discussing and explaining our reasoning and ideas are important for learning, that mathematizing the world around us by examining everyday experiences from a mathematical point of view helps us understand both the world and mathematics better. Teachers can give children stimulating and enjoyable mathematical activities and problems in a nurturing math-talk environment that not only develops children's mathematical thinking but also satisfies children's curiosity, their eagerness to explore and learn, and their desire to engage with their peers and with adults.

In addition to these general processes of representing, reasoning, communicating, connecting, and problem solving, specific mathematical reasoning processes also exist that are important across all topics in mathematics and that mathematics instruction should help children develop. These are—

- *unitizing*—finding or creating a unit, such as seeing 5 ones as a unit of five within six though ten or recognizing that two right triangles with equal legs can make a square and using such squares to make patterns;

- *decomposing and composing*, such as decomposing a rectangle into two squares, or decomposing eight toy dinosaurs into a group of five and a group of three;

- *relating and ordering*, such as putting a collection of trucks in order by length, or determining which collection of bears has more by matching; and

- *looking for patterns and structures and organizing information*, such as noticing that fingers have 5-groups and relating these to 5-groups shown with objects (such as eight toy dinosaurs) or sorting a collection of shapes according to whether they have three sides or four sides.

Examples of such processes have been given in this book for number and geometry. It is vital for parents and teachers to support children in using these mathematical processes.

Throughout this book we have provided snapshots of worthwhile activities for prekindergarten children and some snippets of conversations to illustrate how you might engage children to extend their thinking and draw out mathematical ideas. We end with the suggestion that you revisit some of the examples given here, as well as some activities and environments that you already provide your students, and reconsider these activities with an eye toward engaging children in mathematical processes. Consider how you might further mathematize those activities and environments and enhance your classroom math talk to encourage reasoning, communicating, connecting and representing mathematical ideas, and problem solving. Think about where you can help children unitize, decompose and compose, relate and order, and look for and describe patterns and structures and organize mathematical information. As you do so, consider seeking opportunities throughout the day for the following:

- Have children count objects, actions, and sounds, and discuss with children that counting tells us how many there are.

- Encourage children to reason about how many objects are in a collection, especially when objects are grouped in certain ways (such as a group of five and one more).

- Ask children to compare collections, and encourage reasoning about which has more or less.

- Provide opportunities for children to explore how to combine and take apart shapes or collections of things, and encourage children to discuss and reason about the process.

- Draw children's attention to features, attributes, and sizes of shapes and objects, including their edges, corners, and faces, and discuss how aspects of objects affect such things as whether they roll, stack, or fit in a space.

- Discuss relative locations of objects within the room or building or on the grounds to extend mathematical vocabulary.

Most of all, we encourage you to make learning the important mathematical ideas of early childhood active, engaging, and stimulating, for your students as well as for you.

References

Clements, Douglas H. "Subitizing: What Is It? Why Teach It?" *Teaching Children Mathematics* 5 (March 1999): 400–405.

Clements, Douglas H., and Julie Sarama. "Early Childhood Mathematics Learning." In *Second Handbook of Research on Mathematics Teaching and Learning,* edited by Frank K. Lester, Jr., pp. 461–555. New York: Information Age Publishing, 2007.

———. "Experimental Evaluation of a Research-Based Preschool Mathematics Curriculum." *American Educational Research Journal* 45 (2008): 443–94.

Cross, Christopher T., Taniesha S. Woods, and Heidi Schweingruber, eds. *Mathematics Learning in Early Childhood: Paths Toward Excellence and Equity.* National Research Council, Center for Education, Division of Behavioral and Social Sciences and Education. Washington, D.C.: National Academy Press, 2009.

Fuson, Karen C. *Children's Counting and Concept of Number.* New York: Springer-Verlag, 1988.

———. "Research on Learning and Teaching Addition and Subtraction of Whole Numbers." In *The Analysis of Arithmetic for Mathematics Teaching,* edited by Gaea Leinhardt, Ralph T. Putnam, and Rosemary A. Hattrup, pp. 53–187. Hillsdale, N.J.: Lawrence Erlbaum Associates, 1992a.

———. "Research on Whole Number Addition and Subtraction." In *Handbook of Research on Mathematics Teaching and Learning,* edited by Douglas A. Grouws, pp. 243–75. New York: Macmillan, 1992b.

Kamii, Constance K. *Young Children Reinvent Arithmetic: Implications of Piaget's Theory.* New York: Teachers College Press, 1985.

Kilpatrick, Jeremy, Jane Swafford, and Bradford Findell, eds. *Adding It Up: Helping Children Learn Mathematics.* National Research Council, Mathematics Learning Study Committee, Center for Education, Division of Behavioral and Social Sciences and Education. Washington, D.C.: National Academy Press, 2001.

National Council of Teachers of Mathematics (NCTM). *Curriculum Focal Points for Prekindergarten through Grade 8 Mathematics.* Reston, Va.: NCTM, 2006.

———. *Focus in Kindergarten,* forthcoming.

———. *Focus in Grade 1,* forthcoming.

———. *Focus in Grade 2,* forthcoming.

Piaget, Jean. *The Child's Conception of Number.* New York: W. W. Norton & Co., 1941/1965.

Ramani, Geetha B., and Robert S. Siegler. "Promoting Broad and Stable Improvements in Low Income Children's Numerical Knowledge through Playing Number Board Games." *Child Development* 79 (March–April 2008): 375–94.